W9-DIW-991

The New Assault on Equality

The New
Assault on Equality
IQ and Social Stratification

Edited by

ALAN GARTNER

COLIN GREER

FRANK RIESSMAN

PERENNIAL LIBRARY
Harper & Row, Publishers
New York, Evanston, San Francisco, London

All the essays originally appeared in *Social Policy* with the exception of Frank Riessman's "The Hidden IQ" and David C. McClelland's "Testing for Competence Rather Than 'Intelligence.'"

A hardcover edition of this book is available from Harper & Row, Publishers, Inc.

First PERENNIAL LIBRARY edition published 1974.

LIBRARY OF CONGRESS CATALOG CARD NUMBER: 73-19950

STANDARD BOOK NUMBER: 06-080293-6 (PAPERBACK)

STANDARD BOOK NUMBER: 06-136146-1 (HARDCOVER)

Contents

The New Assault on Equality

The Lingering Infatuation with IQ

Once again intelligence tests are providing the major basis for popular wisdom about education, employment opportunities, and the social class structure. Christopher Jencks's major study, *Inequality: A Reassessment of the Effects of Family and Schooling in America*, accepts IQ scores as a basic measure of cognitive skill. And before Jencks, of course, Arthur Jensen and Richard Herrnstein relied on IQ tests to argue the genetic inferiority of those who perform poorly on them. This despite the evidence of the serious inadequacy of these tests accumulated during the last decade.

In the last fifty years intelligence tests have been used to reinforce public policy that has functioned to limit the opportunities of immigrants, blacks, and third world people. Recently, again, the tests have been brought to the fore to reinforce a diminution of government aid for the schooling of the poor and to further the notion that middle-class individuals do well in the world because of their superior innate intelligence. The fact that the IQ test has again risen as an instrument of conservative policy forces us to reexamine the test and the arguments built around it.

Recall briefly the past twenty years of IQ test research and criticism:

1. A number of experiments have demonstrated quite conclusively that the IQ test score is definitely modifiable, and even Arthur Jensen recognizes that a little "play

therapy" can increase the IQ score by 10 points. The most important experiment, however, was conducted nearly twenty years ago by Ernest Haggard.[1]

Haggard reasoned that although poor children may have taken many IQ tests, they really did not know how to take these tests properly: they lacked meaningful, directed practice. They also lacked motivation, and their relationship to the examiner was typically distant and beset by fears.

Haggard decided to control each of these factors. He gave both poor and middle-class children three one-hour training periods in taking IQ tests. These practice periods included careful explanation of what was involved in each of the different types of problems found on the IQ tests. The explanations were given in words that were familiar to both groups. Haggard also offered special rewards for doing well, and he trained his examiners to be responsive to the deprived children as well as to the middle-class youngsters, thus greatly enhancing the rapport.

Under these conditions the IQs of the disadvantaged children improved dramatically (15 to 20 points on the average). This occurred with only three hours of practice. And it occurred even on the old IQ tests with the middle-class-biased items.

It is noteworthy that the middle-class youngsters improved far less than the deprived youngsters in the Haggard experiment. This is because they were already working nearer their capacity, and the new environmental input—that is the equalization of the test environment, did not lead to the expansion of the gap between the two groups; rather it led to the sharp diminution of the difference.*

*It is noteworthy that Herrnstein and Jensen do not cite the Haggard study in their bibliographies.

1. Ernest A. Haggard, "Social Status and Intelligence," *Genetic Psychology Monographs* 49 (1954): 141–186.

If three hours of motivated practice can make such a difference in performance on the IQ test, one can only imagine what a changed difference in environment on a larger scale would mean for reducing traditional class and ethnic differences. Furthermore, one must be at least a bit suspicious of the high level importance assigned something that can be affected with so little effort.

2. A basic proposition of the IQ thesis is that much of the intelligence it purports to measure is hereditary, and therefore, differences between poor and rich, black and white will not be overcome by improving the environment of the have-nots. The heredity argument greatly depends on a small number of twin studies. These studies attempt to show that identical twins reared apart in different environments will have highly similar IQs because of the identical hereditary structure. But as Leon Kamin[2] has shown, both the studies of separated twins (and the adopted child studies) offer quite insufficient evidence for arguing the primacy of heredity. The most important of the twin studies—those by Sir Cyril Burt—turn out to be problematic in several ways: the separation of the twins was never under experimental control so that degrees of environmental differences are uncertain; Burt's data is dangerously dependent on teachers' subjective assessments of the pupils' intelligence; finally, if intrapair twin differences are considered, then the range of difference expands greatly leaving much room for the potentcy of environmental factors.*

---

*This is not to deny, of course, the role of heredity in affecting cognitive abilities. But we really do not know the way in which heredity does this, how much it does it, how much modifiability is possible, and how much of the difference found between individuals is due to environmental factors. There is no reason not to believe that there are many different cognitive dimensions or

2. Leon Kamin, "Heredity, Intelligence, Politics and Psychology" (Paper delivered at the Annual Meeting, Eastern Psychological Association, Spring 1973.)

Martin Deutsch states this issue well:

A major problem has been that the separation of the twins, like the twinning itself, has not been under the experimentor's control, and therefore the degree of similarity and difference between the environments in which the twins were reared has become an important question. Suffice it to say that enough important and consistent criticisms exist to cast doubt on the definitiveness of the twin data as supportive of any final estimate of the hereditary contribution to intelligence—or to I.Q. One example can make this point. If we examine intrapair *differences*, it is found that mean differences range from 6 to 14 points, and that the *range* of differences is from 0 to 30 points. Such variation between co-twins, *often significantly correlated with environmental differences*, suggests the impact of environment on I.Q. test scores.[3]

3. Whatever it is that the IQ tests measure, it is not self-evident that these are qualities to be highly valued or sought. IQ test results typically do not correlate well with creative thinking.[4] Rather, as Erich Fromm long ago pointed out, they test the quickness of mental adaptability and might better be termed "mental adjustment" tests. They typically measure an individual's ability on brief exercises in which he/she has no intrinsic interest or involvement; they require speed and rapid shifting. By contrast many of the problems that individuals are expected to solve in real life require much time, concentra-

types of cognitive abilities variously affected by hereditary and environmental factors, and that one individual or group may possess more of one type than another. The most important fact is that we do not know. And the use of extremely soft data, loaded with experimental errors, as a basis for establishing presumed hereditary differences in total cognitive ability is misleading.

3. Martin Deutsch, "Heredity and Intelligence" (Paper delivered at the *Social Policy* Conference on IQ, New York, May 1973).

4. See a review of over thirty-eight studies testing this correlation—Michael A. Wallach, *The Intelligence-Creativity Distinction* (General Learning Press, 1971).

tion, and involvement. This type of task is excluded from IQ tests. A strong case can be made that IQ scores are really measuring a very limited, and in some cases, negative type of problem-solving ability.

Originally developed to predict school success, IQ tests do that relatively well.* But since the traditional school learning context is recognized now to be so desperately lacking in either joy or opportunity, the validity of a predictive measure based on the same restrictive and selective values that characterize the school is of dubious efficacy. Indeed one might almost be moved to suggest that lack of success on such tests should be seen as a sign of superior qualities. In any case there seems to be little if any reason to impute to those who perform poorly on the tests inadequate mental heredity.

Bowles and Gintis in this collection have presented a powerful and persuasive argument about the correspondence between the social relations (as well as the performance standards) of the school and world of work and how it is precisely this correspondence that informs the basic character of IQ tests. It is time that their thesis—that the main input of the school is not cognitive but rather attitudinal—for so long disparaged, was taken seriously as a profound jumping off place for social analysis and social action.

Indeed, IQ stands as a contemporary meritocratic illu-

---

*Many persons have made the point in noting the correlation which exists between IQ test scores and social class, that this reflects the fact that it is largely white, urban middle-class persons who make up the tests, share experiences, share a semantic network, and institutional privileges. Deutsch uses the term "cognitive socialization" to describe the test-taking technique, lower anxiety in the testing situation, and greater capability of decoding the specific verbal and written instructions regarding the test on the part of the white, urban, middle-class subjects. He observes that "there is no reason to suppose that any of these factors is central to intellectual ability." Deutsch, "Heredity and Intelligence."

sion mechanism; like the great legend about schools on which our traditional faith in public education is based,[5] it promises the prospect of mobility and social improvement engined by the power of individual abilities unimpeded by class, ethnic, or race discrimination. Instead, however, immobility and stratification defined by class, ethnic, and race variables have been reflected and reinforced by schools and our measure of intelligence. If we set aside both the legend that schools seek to improve cognitive and social status, and the public school's measure of cognitive achievement—the intelligence quotient —it may be possible to recognize that poor performance on the IQ test is an aspect of successfully socialized personalities among poor people. School failure and IQ test failure are aspects of some students having learned well from school and family appropriate styles and goals for their allocated place in society.

It should be no surprise that at a time when the social policy of dominant groups is to curtail mobility, to thwart change, to block redistribution of power and wealth, the IQ test is once again hailed as a valid and objective tool. But IQ as a synonym for cognition is as inaccurate as is the faith in the relation of school, merity, and opportunity itself. And for those who seek to assure opportunity, they must first demythologize the IQ test.

5. See Colin Greer, *The Great School Legend* (New York: Basic Books, 1972).

IQ in the United States Class Structure

SAMUEL BOWLES AND

HERBERT GINTIS

1. INTRODUCTION*

The 1960s and early 1970s have witnessed a sustained political assault against economic inequality in the United States. Blacks, women, welfare recipients, and young rank-and-file workers have brought the issue of inequality into the streets, forced it onto the front pages, and thrown it into the legislature and the courts. The dominant response of the privileged has been concern, tempered by a hardy optimism that social programs could be devised to reduce inequality, alleviate social distress, and bring the nation back from the brink of chaos. This optimism has been at once a reflection of and rooted in a pervasive body of liberal social thought, as codified in

SOURCE: Samuel Bowles and Herbert Gintis, "IQ in the United States Class Structure," *Social Policy* 3, no. 4 and 5 (November-December 1972 and January-February 1973).

*An earlier draft of this paper was presented at the 1972 annual conference of the Union for Radical Political Economics at Webster Springs, West Virginia. We are grateful to participants in those meetings for helpful criticism. We would also like to thank Peter Meyer, Paul Smith, Richard Edwards, Clarence Karier, Michael Reich, David Gordon, Arthur MacEwan, James Campen, and Colin Greer. We have received financial support for this research from the Ford Foundation.

modern mainstream economics and sociology. At the
core of this conventional wisdom in the social sciences is
the conviction that in the advanced capitalist system of
the United States, significant progress toward equality of
economic opportunity can be achieved through a combination of enlightened persuasion and social reforms, particularly in the sphere of education and vocational training.

The disappointing results of the War on Poverty, the
apparent lack of impact of compensatory education, and
in a larger sense the persistence of poverty and racism in
the United States have dented the optimism of the liberal
social scientist and the liberal policy maker alike. The
massive and well-documented failure of the social re-
formers of the 1960s invited a conservative reaction,
most notably in the resurgence of the genetic interpretation of IQ. Sensing the opportunity afforded by the liberal debacle, Arthur Jensen began his celebrated article
on the heritability of IQ with "Compensatory education
has been tried, and apparently it has failed." In the debate that has ensued, an interpretation of the role of IQ
in the class structure has been elaborated: the poor are
poor because they are intellectually incompetent; their
incompetence is particularly intractable because it is
rooted in the genetic structure inherited from their poor
and also intellectually deficient parents.[1] An explanation
of the intergenerational reproduction of the class structure is thus found in the heritability of IQ. The idea is not
new: an earlier wave of genetic interpretations of economic and ethnic inequality followed in the wake of the
purportedly egalitarian but largely unsuccessful educational reforms of the Progressive Era.[2]

1. The most explicit statement of the genetic interpretation of
intergenerational immobility is Richard Herrnstein. "IQ," *Atlantic Monthly,* September 1971, pp. 43–64.
2. Michael Katz notes the historical tendency of genetic interpretations of social inequality to gain popularity following the

The revival of the debate on the genetic interpretation of economic inequality is thus firmly rooted in the fundamental social struggles of the past decade. Yet the debate has been curiously superficial. "The most important thing . . . that we can know about a man," says Louis Wirth, "is what he takes for granted, and the most elemental and important facts about a society are those that are seldom debated and generally regarded as settled."[3] This essay questions the undisputed assumption underlying both sides of the recently revised IQ controversy: that IQ is of basic importance to economic success.

Amid a hundred-page statistical barrage relating to the genetic and environmental components of intelligence, the initiator of the most recent exchange[4] saw fit to devote only three sparse and ambiguous pages to this issue. Later advocates of the "genetic school"[5] have considered this "elemental fact," if anything, less necessary of support. Nor has their choice of battleground proved injudicious: to our knowledge not one of their environmentalist critics has taken the economic importance of IQ any less for granted.[6]

We shall begin this essay with a brief review of the IQ

---

failure of educational reform movements. Michael Katz, *The Irony of Early School Reform* (Cambridge, Mass.: Harvard University Press, 1968). On the rise of the genetic interpretation of inequality toward the end of the Progressive Era, see Clarence J. Karier, "Testing for Order and Control in the Corporate Liberal State," *Educational Theory* 22, no. 2 (Spring 1972).

3. Louis Wirth, Preface, in *Ideology and Utopia: An Introduction to the Sociology of Knowledge,* Karl Mannheim (New York: Harcourt, Brace & World, 1936), pp. x–xxx.

4. Arthur R. Jensen, "How Much Can We Boost IQ and Scholastic Achievement?" *Harvard Educational Review*, Reprint Series, no. 2 (1969), pp. 126–134.

5. For example, H. J. Eysenck, *The IQ Argument* (New York: Library Press, 1971), and Herrnstein, "IQ."

6. For a representative sampling of criticism, see the issues of the *Harvard Educational Review* that followed the Jensen article.

controversy itself, paying special attention to the social consequences of intelligence differentials among races and social classes. This review inspires one highly perplexing question: why have American social scientists so consistently refused to question the actual role of intelligence in occupational success and income determination, in spite of the fact that the empirical data necessary for such an endeavor are well known?

In the third section we shall summarize the results of several years of empirical research into the economic importance of IQ.[7] Our findings, based for the most part on widely available published data, document the fact that IQ is not an important cause of economic success; nor is the inheritance of IQ the reason why rich kids grow up to be rich and poor kids tend to stay poor. The intense debate on the heritability of IQ is thus largely irrelevant to an understanding of poverty, wealth, and inequality of opportunity in the United States.

These results give rise to a host of novel questions—novel in the sense that they would never be asked were the importance of IQ "taken for granted." We shall deal with some of these in succeeding sections of this essay. First, if the social function of IQ distinctions is not status attainment or transmission, what *is* their function? We shall argue in section four that the emphasis on intelligence as the basis for economic success serves to legitimize an authoritarian, hierarchical, stratified, and une-

7. Our work in this area is reported in Herbert Gintis, "Alienation and Power: Toward a Radical Welfare Economics" (Ph.D. diss., Harvard University, 1969); Gintis, "Education and the Characteristics of Worker Productivity," *American Economic Review* 61 (May 1971):266–279; Samuel Bowles, "Schooling and Inequality from Generation to Generation," *Journal of Political Economy* (May-June 1972); Bowles, "The Genetic Inheritance of IQ and the Intergenerational Reproduction of Economic Inequality," Harvard Institute for Economic Research, September 1972.

qual economic system of production, and to reconcile the individual to his or her objective position within this system. Legitimation is enhanced merely when people *believe* in the intrinsic importance of IQ. This belief is facilitated by the strong associations among all the economically desirable attributes—social class, education, cognitive skills, occupational status, and income—and is integrated into a pervasive ideological perspective. Second, if IQ is not a major determinant of social class structure, what is? What are the criteria for admission to a particular social stratum, and what are the sources of intergenerational status transmission? We shall argue in section five that access to an occupational status is contingent upon a pattern of noncognitive personality traits (motivation, orientation to authority, discipline, internalization of work norms), as well as a complex of personal attributes including sex, race, age, and educational credentials through which the individual aids in legitimating and stabilizing the structure of authority in the modern enterprise itself. Thus, primarily because of the central economic role of the school system, the generation of adequate cognitive skills becomes a spin-off, a by-product of a stratification mechanism grounded in the supply, demand, production, and certification of these noncognitive personal attributes.

Finally, we shall comment on the implications of our perspective on the stratification process for political action and social change.

2. THE IQ CONTROVERSY

The argument that differences in genetic endowments are of central and increasing importance in the stratification systems of advanced technological societies has been advanced, in similar forms, by a number of contemporary researchers.[8] At the heart of this argument lies the venerable thesis that IQ, as measured by tests such as the Stanford-Binet, is largely inherited via genetic transmission, rather than molded through environmental influences.*

This thesis bears a short elucidation. That IQ is highly heritable is merely to say that individuals with similar genes will exhibit similar IQs *independent* of differences in the social environments they might experience during their mental development. The main support of the genetic school is several studies of individuals with precisely the same genes (identical twins) raised in different environments (i.e., separated at birth and reared in families with different social statuses). Their IQs tend to be fairly similar.[9] In addition, there are studies of individuals with no common genes (unrelated individuals) raised in the same environment (e.g., the same family) as well as studies of individuals with varying genetic similarities (e.g., fraternal twins, siblings, fathers and sons, aunts and nieces) and varying environments (e.g., siblings raised apart, cousins raised in their respective homes). The difference in IQs for these groups is roughly conformable to the genetic inheritance model suggested by the identical twin and unrelated individual studies.[10]

---

*By IQ we mean—here and throughout this essay—those cognitive capacities that are measured on IQ tests. We have avoided the use of the word "intelligence" as in its common usage it ordinarily connotes a broader range of capacities.

8. Jensen, "How Much Can We Boost IQ"; Carl Bereiter, "The Future of Individual Differences," *Harvard Educational Review*, Reprint Series no. 2 (1969) pp. 162–170; Herrnstein, "IQ"; Eysenck, *The IQ Argument.*
9. Arthur R. Jensen, "Estimation of the Limits of Heritability of Traits by Comparison of Monozygotic and Dizygotic Twins," *Proceedings of the National Academy of Science* 58 (1967):149–157.
10. Jensen, "How Much Can We Boost IQ"; Christopher Jencks et al., *Inequality: A Reassessment of the Effects of Family and Schooling in America* (New York: Basic Books, 1972).

As Eysenck suggests, while geneticists will quibble over
the exact magnitude of heritability of IQ, nearly all will
agree heritability exists and is significant.[11] Environmentalists, while emphasizing the paucity and unrepresenta-
tiveness of the data, have presented rather weak evidence
for their own position and have made little dent in the
genetic position.[12] Unable to attack the central proposition of the genetic school, environmentalists have emphasized that it bears no important social implications.
They have claimed that, although raised in the context of
the economic and educational deprivation of blacks in the
United States, the genetic theory says nothing about the
"necessary" degree of racial inequality or the limits of
compensatory education. First, environmentalists deny
that there is any evidence that the IQ difference between
blacks and whites (amounting to about fifteen IQ points)
is genetic in origin,* and second, they deny that any

11. Eysenck, *The IQ Argument*, p. 9.

12. Jerome S. Kagan, "Inadequate Evidence and Illogical Conclusions," *Harvard Educational Review*, Reprint Series no. 2
(1969) pp. 126–134; J. McV. Hunt, "Has Compensatory Education Failed? Has It Been Attempted?" *Harvard Educational Review*, Reprint Series no. 2 (1969) pp. 130–152.

*Does the fact that a large component of the differences in IQ
among whites is genetic mean that a similar component of the
differences in IQ between blacks and whites is determined by the
former's inferior gene pool? Clearly not. First of all, the degree
of heritability is an *average*, even among whites. For any two
individuals, and *a fortiori*, any two groups of individuals, observed IQ differences may be due to any proportion of genes and
environment—it is required only that they average properly over
the entire population. For instance, *all* of the difference in IQ
between identical twins is environmental, and presumably a
great deal of the difference between adopted brothers is genetic.
Similarly we cannot say whether the average difference in IQ
between Irish and Puerto Ricans is genetic or environmental. In
the case of blacks, however, the genetic school's inference is
even more tenuous. Richard J. Light and Paul V. Smith ("Social
Allocation Models of Intelligence: A Methodological Inquiry,"
Harvard Educational Review 39, no. 3 [August 1969]), have shown

estimate of heritability tells us much about the capacity of "enriched environments" to lessen IQ differentials, either within or between racial groups.*

---

that even accepting Jensen's estimates of the heritability of IQ, the black-white IQ difference could easily be explained by the average environmental differences between the races. Recourse to further experimental investigations will not resolve this issue, for the "conceptual experiments" that would determine the genetic component of black-white differences cannot be performed. Could we take a pair of black identical twins and place them in random environments? Clearly not. Placing a black child in a white home in an overtly racist society will not provide the same "environment" as placing a white child in that house. Similarly looking at the difference in IQs of unrelated black and white children raised in the same home (whether black or white, or mixed) will not tell us the extent of genetic differences, since such children cannot be treated equally, and environmental differences must continue to persist (of course, if in these cases, differences in IQ disappear, the environmentalist case would be supported. But if they do not, no inference can be made).

*Most environmentalists do not dispute Jensen's assertion that existing large-scale compensatory programs have produced dismal results (See Jensen, "How Much Can We Boost IQ," and, for example, Harvey Averch et al., *How Effective is Schooling? A Critical Review and Synthesis of Research Findings* (Santa Monica, Calif.: The RAND Corporation, 1972). But this does not bear on the genetic hypothesis. As Jensen himself notes, the degree of genetic transmission of any trait depends on the various alternative environments that individuals experience. Jensen's estimates of heritability rest *squarely* on the existing array of educational processes and technologies. Any introduction of new social processes of mental development will change the average unstandardized level of IQ, as well as its degree of heritability. For instance, the almost perfect heritability of height is well documented. Yet the average heights of Americans have risen dramatically over the years, due clearly to change in the overall environment. Similarly, whatever the heritability of IQ, the average unstandardized test scores rose 83 percent between 1917 and 1943. See Jencks, *Inequality.*

But compensatory programs are obviously an attempt to change the total array of environments open to children through "educational innovation." While existing large-scale programs appear to have failed to produce significant gains in scholastic achievement, many more innovative, small-scale programs have

But the environmentalists' defense strategy has been
costly. First, plausible, if not logical, inference now lies
on the side of the genetic school, and it's up to environmentalists to "put up or shut up" as to feasible environmental enrichment programs. Second, in their egalitarian
zeal vis-à-vis racial differences, the environmentalists
have sacrificed the modern liberal interpretation of social
stratification. The modern liberal approach is to attribute
social class differences to "unequal opportunity." That is,
while the criteria for economic success are objective and
achievement-oriented, the failures and successes of parents are passed onto their children via distinct learning
and cultural environments. Thus the achievement of a
more equal society merely requires that all youth be
afforded the educational and other social conditions of
the best and most successful.[13] But by focusing on the
environmental differences *between* races, they implicitly
accept that intelligence differences among whites of differing social class background are rooted in differences in
genetic endowments. Indeed the genetic school's data
comes precisely from observed differences in the IQ of
whites across socioeconomic levels! The fundamental
tenet of modern liberal social policy—that "progressive

succeeded. See Carl Bereiter, "The Future of Individual Differences," *Harvard Educational Review*, Reprint Series no. 2 (1969):
pp. 162–170; Charles E. Silberman, *Crisis in the Classroom* (New
York: Random House, 1970); Averch, *How Effective Is Schooling?*
Moreover, even accepting the genetic position should not hinder
us from seeking new environmental innovation—indeed it
should spur us to further creative activities in this direction.
Thus the initial thrust of the genetic school can be at least partially repulsed: there is no reliable evidence either that long-
term contact of blacks with existing white environments would
not close the black-white IQ gap, or that innovative compensatory programs (i.e., programs unlike existing white childrearing
or education environments) might not attenuate or eliminate IQ
differences that are indeed genetic.

13. James S. Coleman et al., *Equality of Educational Opportunity*
(Washington, D.C.: U.S. Government Printing Office, 1966).

social welfare measures" can gradually reduce and eliminate social class differences, cultures of poverty and afflu-
ence, and inequalities of opportunity—seems to be un-
dercut. Thus the "classical liberal" attitude,[14] which
emphasizes that social classes sort themselves out on the
basis of innate individual capacity to cope successfully in
the social environment, and hence tend to reproduce
themselves from generation to generation, is restored.[15]

The vigor of reaction in face of Jensen's argument
indicates the liberals' agreement that IQ is a basic social
determinant (at least ideally) of occupational status and
intergenerational mobility. In Jensen's words, "psychologists' concept of the 'intelligence demands' of an occupation . . . is very much like the general public's concept of
the prestige or 'social standing' of an occupation, and
both are closely related to an independent measure of
. . . occupational status."[16] Jensen continues, quoting O.
D. Duncan: " . . . 'intelligence' . . . is not essentially
different from that of achievement or status in the occupational sphere . . . what we now *mean* by intelligence is
something like the probability of acceptable performance
(given the opportunity) in occupations varying in social
status."[17] Moreover, Jensen argues that the purported
trend toward intelligence's being an increasing require-

14. For example, Edward A. Ross, *Social Control* (New York:
Macmillan, 1924); Louis M. Terman, "The Conservation of Talent," *School and Society* 19, no. 483 (March 1924); Joseph Schumpeter, *Imperialism and Social Classes* (New York: Kelley, 1951).

15. This is not meant to imply that all liberal social theorists
hold the IQ ideology. David McClelland, *The Achieving Society*
(Princeton, N.J.: Van Nostrand, 1967), and Oscar Lewis, "The
Culture of Poverty," *Scientific American* 215 (October 1966):16–
25, among others, explicitly reject IQ as an important determinant of social stratification.

16. Jensen, "Estimation of the Limits of Heritability," p. 14.

17. Otis Dudley Duncan, "Properties and Characteristics of
the Socioeconomic Index," in *Occupations and Social Status,* ed.
Albert J. Reiss (New York: Free Press, 1961), p. 142.

ment for occupational status will continue.[18] This emphasis on the role of intelligence in explaining social stratification is set even more clearly by Carl Bereiter in the
same issue of the *Harvard Educational Review:* "The prospect is of a meritocratic caste system, based . . . on the
natural consequences of inherited differences in intellectual potential. . . . It would tend to persist even though
everyone at all levels of the hierarchy considered it a bad
thing."[19] Something like death and taxes.

Jensen et al. cannot be accused of employing an overly
complicated social theory. Jensen's reason for the "inevitable" association of status and intelligence is that society
"rewards talent and merit," and Herrnstein adds that
society recognizes "the importance and scarcity of intellectual ability."[20] Moreover, the association of intelligence and social class is due to the "screening process,"[21] via education and occupation, whereby each
generation is further refined into social strata on the basis
of IQ. Finally, adds Herrnstein, "new gains of wealth
. . . will increase the IQ gap between upper and lower
classes, making the social ladder even steeper for those
left at the bottom."[22] Herrnstein celebrates the genetic
school's crowning achievement by turning liberal social
policy directly against itself, noting that the heritability of
intelligence and hence the increasing pervasiveness of
social stratification will increase, the more "progressive"
our social policies: "the growth of a virtually hereditary
meritocracy will arise out of the successful realization of
contemporary political and social goals . . . as the environment becomes more favorable for the development of
intelligence, its heritability will increase. . . ."[23] Similarly,
the more we break down discriminatory and ascriptive

18. Jensen, "Estimation of the Limits of Heritability," p. 19.
19. Bereiter, "The Future of Individual Differences," p. 166.
20. Herrnstein, "IQ," p. 51.
21. Jensen, "How Much Can We Boost IQ," p. 75.
22. Herrnstein, "IQ," p. 63.
23. Ibid.

criteria for hiring, the stronger will become the link between IQ and occupational success, and the development
of modern technology can only quicken the process.[24]

Few will be surprised that such statements are made by
the "conservative" genetic school. But why, amid a spir-
ited liberal counterattack in which the minutest details of
the genetic hypothesis are contested and scathingly criticized, is the validity of the genetic school's description of
the social function of intelligence blandly accepted? The
widespread agreement among participants in the debate
that IQ is an important determinant of economic success
can hardly be explained by compelling empirical evidence adduced in support of the position. Quite the contrary. As we will show in the next section, the available
data point strongly to the unimportance of IQ in getting
ahead economically. In Section 4 we shall argue that the
actual function of IQ testing and its associated ideology
is that of legitimizing the stratification system, rather than
generating it. The treatment of IQ in many strands of
liberal sociology and economics merely reflects its actual
function in social life: the legitimization and rationaliza-
tion of the existing social relations of production.

3. THE IMPORTANCE OF IQ

The most immediate support for the IQ theory of social
stratification—which we will call IQ-ism—flows from the
strong association of IQ and economic success. This is
illustrated in Table 1, which exhibits the probability of
achieving any particular decile in the economic success
distribution for an individual whose adult IQ lies in a
specified decile.*

*In Table 1, as throughout this paper, "adult IQ" is measured
by scores on a form of the Armed Forces Qualification Test. This

24. Ibid.

The data, most of which was collected by the United States Census Current Population Survey in 1962, refer to "non-Negro" males, aged twenty-five to thirty-four, from nonfarm background in the experienced labor force. We have chosen this population because it represents the dominant labor force and the group into which minority groups and women would have to integrate to realize the liberal ideal of equal opportunity, and hence to whose statistical associations these groups would become subject. The data relating to childhood IQ and adult IQ are from a 1966 survey of veterans by the National Opinion Research Center and the California Guidance Study.[25] The quality of the data preclude any claims to absolute precision in our estimation. Yet our main

---

measure is strongly affected both by early IQ (in this paper measured by Stanford-Binet or its equivalent at age six to eight) and years of schooling, and hence can be considered a measure of adult cognitive achievement. Economic success is measured throughout as the average of an individual's income and the social prestige of his occupation as measured on the Duncan occupational status index, each scaled to have standard deviation equal to one. See Duncan, "Properties and Characteristics of the Socioeconomic Index." For a description of the independent behavior of income and status, see Bowles, "The Genetic Inheritance of IQ and the Intergenerational Reproduction of Economic Inequality." We have chosen a weighted average for simplicity of exposition, and in recognition of their joint importance in a reasonable specification of economic success.

25. See Peter Blau and Otis Dudley Duncan, *The American Occupational Structure* (New York: John Wiley, 1967); Otis Dudley Duncan, David L. Featherman, and Beverly Duncan, *Socioeconomic Background and Occupational Achievement: Extensions of a Basic Model*, Final Report Project No. 5-0074 (EO-191), Contract No. OE-5-85-072 (Washington, D.C.: U.S. Department of Health, Education, and Welfare, Office of Education, Bureau of Research, 1968); Bowles, "Schooling and Inequality from Generation to Generation"; and Bowles, "The Genetic Inheritance of IQ," for a more complete description. Similar calculations for other age groups yield results consistent with our three main empirical propositions.

propositions remain supported, even making allowance for substantive degrees of error. We must emphasize, however, that the validity of our basic propositions does not depend on our particular data set. While we believe our data base to be the most representative and careful construction from available sources,* we have checked

*A further word is in order on Tables 1 through 7. Most popular discussions of the relation of IQ and economic success (e.g., Jensen, *"How Much Can We Boost IQ"*; Herrnstein, "IQ"; Jencks, *Inequality*) present statistical material in terms of "correlation coefficients" and "contribution to explained variance." We believe that these technical expressions convey little information to the reader not thoroughly initiated in their use and interpretation. The concept of differential probability embodied in Tables 1 through 7, we feel, is operationally more accessible to the reader, and dramatically reveals the patterns of mobility and causality only implicit in summary statistics of the correlation variety.

Let us repeat, Tables 1 through 7 have *not* been constructed by directly observing the decile position of individuals on each of the various variables and recording the percentages in each cell of the relevant table. This approach is impossible for two reasons. First, such statistics are simply unavailable on the individual level. As we have noted, our statistical base embraces the findings of several distinct data sources, no single one of which includes all the variables used in our analysis. Second, for certain technical reasons (e.g., errors in variables and restrictions of range), correction factors must be applied to the raw data before they can be used for analysis. These general issues are discussed in Jencks, *Inequality,* and with respect to our data, in Bowles, "The Genetic Inheritance of IQ and the Intergenerational Reproduction of Economic Inequality," and Gintis, "Education and the Characteristics of Worker Productivity."

Tables 1 through 7 are constructed by making explicit certain assumptions that are only implicit, but absolutely necessary to the correlational arguments of Jensen and others. These assumptions include the linearity of the relations among all variables and the approximate normality of their joint probability distribution. Our statistical technique, then, is standard linear regression analysis, with correlations, regression coefficients, and path coefficients represented in their (mathematically equivalent) tabular form.

TABLE 1[a] **Probability of Attainment of Different Levels of Economic Success for Individuals of Differing Levels of Adult IQ, by Deciles**

Adult IQ by Deciles

x y	10	9	8	7	6	5	4	3	2	1
10	30.9	19.8	14.4	10.9	8.2	6.1	4.4	3.0	1.7	0.6
9	19.2	16.9	14.5	12.4	10.5	8.7	7.0	5.4	3.6	1.7
8	13.8	14.5	13.7	12.6	11.4	10.1	8.7	7.1	5.3	2.8
7	10.3	12.4	12.6	12.3	11.7	11.0	10.0	8.7	7.0	4.1
6	7.7	10.4	11.4	11.7	11.8	11.5	11.0	10.1	8.7	5.7
5	5.7	8.7	10.1	11.0	11.5	11.8	11.7	11.4	10.4	7.7
4	4.1	7.0	8.7	10.0	11.0	11.7	12.3	12.6	12.4	10.3
3	2.8	5.3	7.1	8.7	10.1	11.4	12.6	13.7	14.5	13.8
2	1.7	3.6	5.4	7.0	8.7	10.5	12.4	14.5	16.9	19.2
1	0.6	1.7	3.0	4.4	6.1	8.2	10.9	14.4	19.8	30.9

Economic Success by Deciles (row axis label)

[a]*Table 1 corresponds to a correlation coefficient $r = .52$.*
Example of use: For an individual in the 85th percentile in Adult IQ (x = 9), the probability of attaining between the 20th and 30th percentile in Economic Success is 5.3 percent (the entry in column 9, row 3).

our results against several other data bases, including Jencks, Hauser, Lutterman, and Sewell, Conlisk, Griliches and Mason, and Duncan and Featherman.[26]

26. Jencks, *Inequality;* Robert Hauser, Kenneth G. Lutterman, and William H. Sewell, "Socioeconomic Background and the Earnings of High School Graduates" (manuscript, University of Wisconsin, August 1971); John Conlisk, "A Bit of Evidence on the Income-Education-Ability Interaction," *Journal of Human Resources* 6 (Summer 1971):358–362; Zvi Griliches and William M. Mason, "Education, Income, and Ability," *Journal of Political Economy* 80, no. 3 (May-June 1972); Otis Dudley Duncan and David L. Featherman, "Psychological and Cultural Factors in the Process of Occupational Achievement," Population Studies Center, University of Michigan, 1971.

When corrections are made for measurement error and restriction of range (see Bowles[27] and Jencks), statistical analysis of each of these data bases strongly supports all of our major propositions.

The interpretation of table 1 is straightforward. The entries in the table are calculated directly from the simple correlation coefficient between our variables adult IQ and economic success. In addition to reporting the correlation coefficient, we have described these data in tabular form as in table 1 to illustrate the meaning of the correlation coefficient in terms of the differing probability of economic success for people at various positions in the distribution of IQs. We cannot stress too strongly that while the correlation coefficients in this and later tables are estimated from the indicated data, the entries in the table represent nothing more than a simple translation of their correlations, using assumptions that—through virtually universally employed in this kind of research—substantially simplify the complexity of the actual data. Now, turning to the table, we can see, for example, that a correlation between these two variables of .52 implies that an individual whose adult IQ lies in the top 10 percent of the population has a probability of 30.9 percent of ending up in the top tenth of the population in economic success, and a probability of 0.6 percent of ending up in the bottom tenth. Since an individual chosen at random will have a probability of 10 percent of ending up in any decile of economic success, we can conclude that being in the top decile in IQ renders an individual (white male) 3.09 times as likely to be in the top economic success decile, and .06 times as likely to end up in the bottom, as would be predicted by chance. Each of the remaining entries in Table 1 can be interpreted correspondingly.

Yet Tables 2 and 3, which exhibit the corresponding

27. Bowles, "The Genetic Inheritance of IQ."

TABLE 2[a] Probability of Attainment of Different Levels of Economic Success for Individuals of Differing Levels of Education, by Deciles

Years of Schooling by Deciles

x / y	10	9	8	7	6	5	4	3	2	1
10	37.6	22.3	14.6	9.8	6.6	4.3	2.6	1.4	0.6	0.1
9	20.9	19.5	16.2	13.1	10.3	7.9	5.7	3.8	2.1	0.6
8	13.5	16.1	15.3	13.8	12.0	10.1	8.0	5.9	3.7	1.4
7	9.1	13.0	13.8	13.6	12.8	11.6	10.0	8.0	5.6	2.5
6	6.1	10.2	12.0	12.8	12.9	12.5	11.6	10.1	7.8	4.0
5	4.0	7.8	10.1	11.6	12.5	12.9	12.8	12.0	10.2	6.1
4	2.5	5.6	8.0	10.0	11.6	12.8	13.6	13.8	13.0	9.1
3	1.4	3.7	5.9	8.0	10.1	12.0	13.8	15.3	16.1	13.5
2	0.6	2.1	3.8	5.7	7.9	10.3	13.1	16.2	19.5	20.9
1	0.1	0.6	1.4	2.6	4.3	6.6	9.8	14.6	22.3	37.6

Economic Success by Deciles (row label, left axis)

[a]*Table 2 corresponds to a correlation coefficient $r = .63$.*
Example of use: For an individual in the 85th percentile in Education $(x = 9)$, the probability of attaining between the 20th and 30th percentiles in Economic Success $(y = 3)$ is 3.7 percent (the entry in column 9, row 3).

probabilities of economic success given number of years of schooling and level of socioeconomic background,* show that this statistical support is surely misleading: even stronger associations appear between years of schooling and economic success, as well as between social background and economic success. For example, being in the top decile in years of schooling renders an

---

*In Table 3, as throughout this paper, socioeconomic background is measured as a weighted sum of parental income, father's occupational status, and father's income, where the weights are chosen so as to produce the maximum multiple correlation with economic success.

individual 3.76 times as likely to be at the top of the economic heap, and .01 times as likely to be at the bottom, while the corresponding ratios are 3.26 and .04 for social background. It is thus quite possible to draw from aggregate statistics, equally cogently, both an "educational attainment theory" of social stratification and a "socioeconomic background" theory. Clearly there are logical errors in all such facile inferences.

Of course, the IQ proponent will argue that there is no real problem here: the association of social class background and economic success follows from the importance of IQ to economic success, and the fact that individuals of higher class background have higher IQ. Similarly one may argue that the association of education and economic success follows from the fact that education simply picks out and develops the talents of intelligent individuals. The problem is that equally cogent arguments can be given for the primacy of either education or social class, and the corresponding subordinateness of the others. The above figures are equally compatible with all three interpretations.

In this section we shall show that all three factors (IQ, social class background, and education) contribute independently to economic success, but that IQ is by far the least important. Specifically we will demonstrate the truth of the following three propositions, which constitute the empirical basis of our thesis concerning the unimportance of IQ in generating the class structure.

First, although higher IQs and economic success tend to go together, higher IQs are not an important cause of economic success. The statistical association between adult IQ and economic success, while substantial, derives largely from the common association of both of these variables with social class background and level of schooling. Thus to appraise the economic importance of IQ, we must focus attention on family and school.

Second, although higher levels of schooling and economic success

TABLE 3[a] **Probability of Attainment of Different Levels of Economic Success for Individuals of Differing Levels of Social Class Background**

Social Class Background by Deciles

x y	10	9	8	7	6	5	4	3	2	1
10	32.6	20.4	14.5	10.7	7.8	5.7	3.9	2.5	1.4	0.4
9	19.7	17.5	14.9	12.6	10.5	8.5	6.7	5.0	3.2	1.3
8	13.8	14.9	14.1	12.9	11.6	10.1	8.6	6.9	4.9	2.4
7	10.0	12.5	12.9	12.6	12.0	11.1	10.0	8.5	6.7	3.7
6	7.3	10.4	11.5	12.0	12.0	11.7	11.1	10.1	8.5	5.3
5	5.3	8.5	10.1	11.1	11.7	12.0	12.0	11.5	10.4	7.3
4	3.7	6.7	8.5	10.0	11.1	12.0	12.6	12.9	12.5	10.0
3	2.4	4.9	6.9	8.6	10.1	11.6	12.9	14.1	14.9	13.8
2	1.3	3.2	5.0	6.7	8.5	10.5	12.6	14.9	17.5	19.7
1	0.4	1.4	2.5	3.9	5.7	7.8	10.7	14.5	20.4	32.6

Economic Success by Deciles

[a]*Table 3 corresponds to a correlation coefficient r = .55.*
Example of use: For an individual in the 85th percentile in Social Class (x = 9), the probability of attaining between the 20th and the 30th percentile in Economic Success (y = 3) is 4.9 percent (the entry in column 9, row 3).

likewise tend to go together, the intellectual abilities developed or certified in school make little causal contribution to getting ahead economically. Thus only a minor portion of the substantial statistical association between schooling and economic success can be accounted for by the schools' role in producing or screening cognitive skills. The predominant economic function of schools must therefore involve the accreditation of individuals, as well as the production and selection of personality traits and other personal attributes rewarded by the economic system. Our third proposition asserts a parallel result with respect to the effect of social class background.

Third, the fact that economic success tends to run in the family arises almost completely independently from any genetic inheritance of IQ. Thus, while one's economic status tends to resemble that of one's parents, only a minor portion of this association can be attributed to social class differences in childhood IQ, and a virtually negligible portion to social class differences in genetic endowments, even accepting the Jensen estimates of heritability. Thus a perfect equalization of IQs across social classes would reduce the intergenerational transmission of economic status by a negli-

TABLE 4[a] **Differential Probabilities of Attaining Economic Success for Individuals of Equal Levels of Education and Social Class Background, but Differing Levels of Adult IQ**

Adult IQ by Deciles

x y	10	9	8	7	6	5	4	3	2	1
10	14.1	12.3	11.4	10.7	10.1	9.6	9.0	8.5	7.8	6.6
9	12.4	11.4	10.9	10.5	10.2	9.8	9.5	9.1	8.6	7.7
8	11.4	10.9	10.6	10.4	10.2	9.9	9.7	9.4	9.1	8.4
7	10.7	10.5	10.4	10.3	10.1	10.0	9.9	9.7	9.5	9.0
6	10.1	10.2	10.2	10.1	10.1	10.1	10.0	9.9	9.8	9.5
5	9.5	9.8	9.9	10.0	10.1	10.1	10.1	10.2	10.2	10.1
4	9.0	9.5	9.7	9.9	10.0	10.1	10.3	10.4	10.5	10.7
3	8.4	9.1	9.4	9.7	9.9	10.2	10.4	10.6	10.9	11.4
2	7.7	8.6	9.1	9.5	9.8	10.2	10.5	10.9	11.4	12.4
1	6.6	7.8	8.5	9.0	9.6	10.1	10.7	11.4	12.3	14.1

Economic Success by Deciles (vertical axis label, y)

[a]*Table 4 corresponds to a standardized regression coefficient $\beta = .13$. Example of use: Suppose two individuals have the same levels of Education and Social Class Background, but one is in the 85th percentile in Adult IQ (x = 9), while the other is in the 15th decile in Adult IQ (x = 2). Then the first individual is $10.9/9.1 = 1.2$ times as likely as the second to attain the 8th decile in Economic Success (column 9, row 8, divided by column 2, row 8).*

gible amount. We conclude that a family's position in the class structure is reproduced primarily by mechanisms operating independently of the inheritance, production, and certification of intellectual skills.

Our statistical technique for the demonstration of these propositions will be that of linear regression analysis. This technique allows us to derive numerical estimates of the independent contribution of each of the separate but correlated influences (social class background, childhood IQ, years of schooling, adult IQ) on economic success, by answering the question: what is the magnitude of the association between any one of these influences among individuals who are equal on some or all the others? Equivalently it answers the question: what are the probabilities of attaining particular deciles in economic success among individuals who are in the same decile in some or all of the above influences but one, and in varying deciles in this one variable alone?

The IQ argument is based on the assumption that social background and education are related to economic success *because* they are associated with higher adult cognitive skills. Table 4 shows this to be essentially incorrect. Table 4, by exhibiting the relation between adult IQ and economic success among individuals with the same social class background and level of schooling, shows that the IQ-economic success association exhibited in Table 1 is largely a by-product of these more basic social influences. That is, for a given level of social background and schooling, differences in adult IQ add very little to our ability to predict eventual economic success. Thus, for example, an individual with an average number of years of schooling and an average socioeconomic family background, but with a level of cognitive skill to place him in the top decile of the IQ distribution, has a probability of 14.1 percent of attaining the highest economic success decile. This figure may be compared with 10 percent, the analogous probability for an individual with average levels of

IQ as well as schooling and social background. Our first proposition—that the relation between IQ and economic success is not causal, but rather operates largely through the effects of the correlated variables, years of schooling and social class background—is thus strongly supported.* We are thus led to focus directly on the role of social class background and schooling in promoting economic success.

Turning first to schooling, the argument of the IQ proponents is that the strong association between level of schooling and economic success exhibited in Table 2 is due to the fact that economic success depends on cognitive capacities, and schooling both selects individuals with high intellectual ability for further training and then develops this ability into concrete adult cognitive skills. Table 5 shows this view to be false. This table exhibits the effect of schooling on chances for economic success, for individuals who have the same adult IQ. Comparing Table 5 with Table 2, we see that cognitive differences account for a negligible part of schooling's influence on economic success: individuals with similar levels of adult IQ but differing levels of schooling have substantially different chances of economic success. Indeed the similarity of Tables 2 and 5 demonstrates the validity of our second porposition—that schooling affects chances of economic success predominantly by the noncognitive traits which it generates, or on the basis of which it selects individuals for higher education.[28]

---

*This is not to say that IQ is never an important criteria of success. We do not contend that extremely low or high IQs are irrelevant to economic failure or success. Now do we deny that for some individuals or for some jobs, cognitive skills are economically important. Rather, we assert that for the vast majority of workers and jobs, selection, assessed job adequacy, and promotion are based on attributes other than IQ.

28. For a more extensive treatment of this point, using data from nine independent samples, see Gintis, "Education and the Characteristics of Worker Productivity."

TABLE 5[a] Differential Probabilities of Attaining Economic Success for Individuals of Equal Adult IQ but Differing Levels of Education

Years of Schooling by Deciles

x y	10	9	8	7	6	5	4	3	2	1
10	33.2	20.6	14.6	10.6	7.7	5.5	3.8	2.4	1.3	0.4
9	19.9	17.8	15.1	12.7	10.5	8.5	6.6	4.8	3.1	1.2
8	13.8	15.0	14.2	13.0	11.6	10.1	8.5	6.8	4.8	2.3
7	9.9	12.6	13.0	12.7	12.1	11.2	10.0	8.5	6.6	3.5
6	7.2	10.4	11.6	12.1	12.1	11.8	11.2	10.1	8.4	5.1
5	5.1	8.4	10.1	11.2	11.8	12.1	12.1	11.6	10.4	7.2
4	3.5	6.6	8.5	10.0	11.2	12.1	12.7	13.0	12.6	9.9
3	2.3	4.8	6.8	8.5	10.1	11.6	13.0	14.2	15.0	13.8
2	1.2	3.1	4.8	6.6	8.5	10.5	12.7	15.1	17.8	19.9
1	0.4	1.3	2.4	3.8	5.5	7.7	10.6	14.6	20.6	33.2

Economic Success by Deciles

[a] *Table 5 corresponds to a standardized regression coefficient $\beta = .56$. Example of use: Suppose two individuals have the same Adult IQ, but one is in the 9th decile in Level of Education $(x = 9)$, while the other is in the 2nd decile $(x = 2)$. Then the first individual is $15.0/4.8 = 3.12$ times as likely as the second to attain the 8th decile in Economic Success (column 9, row 8, divided by column 2, row 8).*

The next step in our argument is to show that the relationship between social background and economic success operates almost entirely independently of individual differences in IQ. Whereas Table 3 exhibits the total effect of social class on an individual's economic success, Table 6 exhibits the same effect among individuals with the same childhood IQ. Clearly these tables are nearly identical. That is, even were all social class differences in IQ eliminated, a similar pattern of social class intergenerational immobility would result.[29] Our third proposition is thus supported: the intergenerational

29. For a more extensive demonstration of this proposition, see Bowles, "The Genetic Inheritance of IQ."

TABLE 6[a] **Differential Probabilities of Attaining Economic Success for Individuals of Equal Early IQ but Differing Levels of Social Class Background**

Social Class Background by Deciles

x → / y ↓	10	9	8	7	6	5	4	3	2	1
10	27.7	18.5	14.1	11.1	8.8	6.9	5.3	3.9	2.5	1.1
9	18.2	15.8	13.8	12.1	10.5	9.0	7.6	6.1	4.5	2.4
8	13.7	13.8	13.0	12.1	11.1	10.1	8.9	7.6	6.1	3.7
7	10.7	12.0	12.1	11.8	11.3	10.7	9.9	8.9	7.5	5.0
6	8.4	10.5	11.1	11.3	11.3	11.1	10.7	10.0	9.0	6.6
5	6.6	9.0	10.0	10.7	11.1	11.3	11.3	11.1	10.5	8.4
4	5.0	7.5	8.9	9.9	10.7	11.3	11.8	12.1	12.0	10.7
3	3.7	6.1	7.6	8.9	10.1	11.1	12.1	13.0	13.8	13.7
2	2.4	4.5	6.1	7.6	9.0	10.5	12.1	13.8	15.8	18.2
1	1.1	2.5	3.9	5.3	6.9	8.8	11.1	14.1	18.5	27.7

Economic Success by Deciles (left axis label)

[a]*Table 6 corresponds to a standardized regression coefficient $\beta = .46$. Example of use: Suppose two individuals have the same Childhood IQ, but one is in the 9th decile in Social Background, while the other is in the 2nd decile. Then the first is $18.5/2.5 = 7.4$ times as likely as the second to attain the top decile in Economic Success (column 9, row 10, divided by column 2, row 10).*

transmission of social and economic status operates primarily via noncognitive mechanisms, despite the fact that the school system rewards higher IQ—an attribute significantly associated with higher social class background.

The unimportance of the specifically genetic mechanism operating via IQ in the intergenerational reproduction of economic inequality is even more striking. Table 7 exhibits the degree of association between social class background and economic success that can be attributed to the genetic inheritance of IQ alone. This table assumes that all direct influences of socioeconomic background upon economic success have been eliminated, and that the noncognitive components of schooling's contribution to economic success are eliminated as well (the perfect meritocracy based on intellectual ability). On the other hand, it assumes Jensen's estimate for the degree of heritability of IQ. A glance at table 7 shows that the resulting level of intergenerational inequality in this highly hypothetical example would be negligible.

The unimportance of IQ in explaining the relation between social class background and economic success, and the unimportance of cognitive achievement in explaining the contribution of schooling to economic success, together with our previously derived observation that most of the association between IQ and economic success can be accounted for by the common association of these variables with education and social class, support our major assertion: IQ is not an important intrinsic criterion for economic success. Our data thus hardly lend credence to Duncan's assertion that " 'intelligence' . . . is not essentially different from that of achievement or status in the occupational sphere,"[30] nor to Jensen's belief in the "inevitable" association of status and intelligence, based on society's "rewarding talent and merit,"[31] nor to Herrnstein's dismal prognostication of a "virtually hereditary meritocracy" as the fruit of successful liberal reform in an advanced industrial society.[32]

30. Duncan, "Properties and Characteristics of the Socioeconomic Index."

31. Jensen, "Estimation of the Limits of Heritability," p. 73.

32. Herrnstein, "IQ," p. 63.

4. IQ AND THE LEGITIMATION OF THE HIERARCHICAL DIVISION OF LABOR

A Preview

We have disputed the view that IQ is an important causal antecedent of economic success. Yet IQ clearly plays an important role in the U.S. stratification system. In this

TABLE 7[a] The Genetic Component of Intergenerational Status Transmission, Assuming the Jensen Heritability Coefficient, and Assuming Education Operates Via Cognitive Mechanisms Alone

Social Class Background by Deciles

x	10	9	8	7	6	5	4	3	2	1
10	10.6	10.3	10.2	10.1	10.0	10.0	9.9	9.8	9.7	9.4
9	10.4	10.2	10.1	10.1	10.0	10.0	9.9	9.9	9.8	9.6
8	10.2	10.1	10.1	10.1	10.0	10.0	9.9	9.9	9.9	9.8
7	10.1	10.1	10.1	10.0	10.0	10.0	10.0	9.9	9.9	9.9
6	10.0	10.0	10.0	10.0	10.0	10.0	10.0	10.0	10.0	10.0
5	10.0	10.0	10.0	10.0	10.0	10.0	10.0	10.0	10.0	10.0
4	9.9	9.9	9.9	10.0	10.0	10.0	10.0	10.1	10.1	10.1
3	9.8	9.9	9.9	9.9	10.0	10.0	10.1	10.1	10.1	10.2
2	9.6	9.8	9.9	9.9	10.0	10.0	10.1	10.1	10.2	10.4
1	9.4	9.7	9.8	9.9	10.0	10.0	10.1	10.2	10.3	10.6

y axis label: *Economic Success by Deciles*

[a]*Table 7 corresponds to .02 standard deviations difference in Economic Success per standard deviation difference in Social Class Background, in a causal model assuming Social Class Background affects Early IQ only via genetic transmission, and assuming Economic Success is directly affected only by cognitive variables.*

Example of use: For an individual in the 85th percentile in Social Class Background (x = 9), the probability of attaining between the 20th and 30th percentiles in Economic Success (y = 3), assuming only genetic and cognitive mechanisms, is 10.1 percent (the entry in column 9, row 8.

section we shall argue that the set of beliefs surrounding IQ betrays its true function—that of legitimating the social institutions underpinning the stratification system itself.

Were the IQ ideology correct, understanding the ramifications of cognitive differences would require our focusing on the technical relations of production in an advanced technological economy. Its failure, however, bids us scrutinize a different aspect of production—its social relations. By the "social relations of production" we mean the system of rights and responsibilities, duties and rewards, that governs the interaction of all individuals involved in organized productive activity.[33] In the following section we shall argue that the social relations of production determine the major attributes of the U.S. stratification system.[34] Here, however, we shall confine ourselves to the proposition that the IQ ideology is a major factor in legitimating these social relations in the consciousness of workers.

The social relations of production in different societies are quite diverse; they lay the basis for such divergent stratification systems as communal-reciprocity, caste, feudal serf, slave, community-collective, and wage labor of capitalist and state socialist varieties. In advanced capitalist society the stratification system is based on what we term the hierarchical division of labor, characterized by

33. For an explication of the social relations of production, see Andre Gorz, "Capitalist Relations of Production and the Socially Necessary Labor Force," in *All We Are Saying . . .* , ed. Arthur Lothstein (New York: G. P. Putnam's, 1970), and Herbert Gintis, "Power and Alienation," in *Readings in Political Economy*, ed. James Weaver (Boston: Allyn and Bacon, forthcoming).

34. See Bowles, "Unequal Education and the Reproduction of the Social Division of Labor," *Review of Radical Political Economy* 3 (Fall-Winter 1971); Bowles, "Contradictions in U.S. Higher Education," in *Readings in Political Economy*, ed. James Weaver (Boston: Allyn and Bacon, forthcoming), for an explanation of the connection between the social relations of production and the stratification system.

power and control emanating from the top downward through a finely graduated bureaucratic order.[35] The distribution of economic reward and social privilege in the United States is an expression of the hierarchical division of labor within the enterprise.

In this section, then, we shall show that the IQ ideology serves to legitimate the hierarchical division of labor. First, we argue that such legitimation is necessary because capitalist production is "totalitarian" in a way only vaguely adumbrated in other social spheres—family, interpersonal relations, law, and politics. Indeed history exhibits periodic onslaughts upon the hierarchical division of labor, and its acceptance is always problematic. Second, we argue that the IQ ideology is conducive to a general technocratic and meritocratic view of the stratification system that tends to legitimate these social relations, as well as its characteristic means of allocating individuals to various levels of the hierarchy. Third, we argue that the IQ ideology operates to reconcile workers to their eventual economic positions primarily via the schooling experience, with its putative objectivity, meritocratic orientation, and technical efficiency in supplying the cognitive needs of the labor force. Fourth, we shall argue that the use of both formal education and the IQ ideology was not merely a historical accident but arose through the conscious policies of capitalists and their intellectual servants to perform the functions indicated above.

35. On the origins and functions of the hierarchical division of labor, see Stephen Marglin, "What Do Bosses Do?" (manuscript, Department of Economics, Harvard University, 1971); Richard C. Edwards, "Alienation and Inequality: Capitalist Relations of Production in a Bureaucratic Enterprise" (Ph.D. diss., Harvard University, July 1972); Max Weber, *From Max Weber: Essays in Sociology* (New York: Oxford University Press, 1946); Chester I. Barnard, *The Functions of the Executive* (Cambridge: Harvard University Press, 1938). A similar hierarchy in production occurs in state socialist countries.

The Need for Legitimacy

If one takes for granted the basic economic organization of society, its members need only be equipped with adequate cognitive and operational skills to fulfill work requirements, and provided with a reward structure motivating individuals to acquire and supply these skills. United States capitalism accomplishes the first of these requirements through family, school, and on-the-job training, and the second through a wage structure patterned after the job hierarchy.

But the social relations of production cannot be taken for granted. The bedrock of the capitalist economy is the legally sanctioned power of the directors of an enterprise to organize production, to determine the rules that regulate worker's productive activities, and to hire and fire accordingly, with only moderate restriction by workers' organizations and government regulations. But this power cannot be taken for granted and can be exercised forcefully against violent opposition only sporadically. Violence alone, observe Lassevell and Kaplan, is inadequate as a stable basis for the possession and exercise of power, and they appropriately quote Rousseau: "The strongest man is never strong enough to be always master, unless he transforms his power into right, and obedience into duty." Where the assent of the less favored cannot be secured by power alone, it must be part of a total process whereby the existing structure of work roles and their allocation among individuals are seen as ethically acceptable and even technically necessary.

In some social systems the norms that govern the economic system are quite similar to those governing other major social spheres. Thus in feudal society the authority of the lord of the manor is not essentially different from that of the political monarch, the church hierarchy, or the

family patriarch, and the ideology of "natural estates"
suffuses all social activity. No special normative order is
required for the economic system. But in capitalist society, to make the hierarchical division of labor appear
just is no easy task, for the totalitarian organization of the
enterprise clashes sharply with the ideals of equality,
democracy, and participation that pervade the political
and legal spheres. Thus the economic enterprise as a
political dictatorship and a social caste system requires
special legitimation, and the mechanisms used to place
individuals in unequal (and unequally rewarding) positions require special justification.

Indeed the history of U.S. labor is studded with revolts
against the hierarchical division of labor, particularly
prior to the full development of formal education and the
IQ ideology in the early twentieth century.[36]

In 1844 the Lynn, Mass., shoe workers, losing control
over their craft and their labor in the face of the rising
factory system, wrote in their "Declaration of Indepen-
dence":

Whereas, our employers have robbed us of certain rights
. . . we feel bound to rise unitedly in our strength and
burst asunder as Freemen ought the shackles and fetters
with which they have long been chaining and binding us,
by an unjust and unchristian use of power . . . which the
possession of capital and superior knowledge fur-
nishes.[37]

The ideology of the dispossessed farmer in the 1880s and
1890s or of the bankrupted small shopkeeper after the
turn of the century is little different. That these radical
thrusts against the hierarchical division of labor have by

36. We are presently witnessing a revival of such revolts with
the partial breakdown of this ideology. See Judson Gooding,
"Blue Collar Blues on the Assembly Line," *Fortune,* July 1970;
Gooding, "The Fraying White Collar," *Fortune,* December 1970.

37. Quoted in Norman Ware, *The Industrial Worker: 1840–1860*
(New York, 1964), p. 42.

and large been deflected into more manageable wage or
status demands bespeaks the power of the capitalist system to legitimize its changing structure, but in no way
suggests that the perpetuation of the capitalist relations
of production was ever a foregone conclusion.[38]

The Thrust of Legitimation: IQ, Technocracy, and Meritocracy

We may isolate several related aspects of the social relations of production that are legitimized in part by the IQ
ideology. To begin there are the overall characteristics of
work in advanced United States capitalism: bureaucratic
organization, hierarchical lines of authority, job fragmentation, and unequal reward. It is highly essential that the
individual accept, and indeed come to see as natural,
these undemocratic and unequal aspects of the workaday
world.

Moreover, the mode of allocating individuals to these
various positions in United States capitalism is characterized by intense competition in the educational system
followed by individual assessment and choice by employers. Here again the major problem is that this "allocation
mechanism" must appear egalitarian in process and just
in outcome, parallel to the formal principle of "equality
of all before the law" in a democratic juridical system
based on freedom of contract.

While these two areas refer to the legitimation of capitalism as a social system, they have their counterpart in

38. For contemporary discussions of the feasibility of significant alternatives to the hierarchical division of labor, see Paul
Blumberg, *Industrial Democracy* (New York: Schocken Books,
1969); Carole Pateman, *Participation and Democratic Theory* (Cambridge, Mass.: Cambridge University Press, 1970); Murray Book-
chin, *Post-Scarcity Anarchism* (Berkeley: Ramparts Press, 1971);
Gintis, "Power and Alienation."

the individual's personal life. Thus, just as individuals must come to accept the overall social relations of production, workers must respect the authority and competence of their own "superiors" to direct their activities, and justify their own authority (however extensive) over others. Similarly, just as the overall system of role allocation must be legitimized, so individuals must assent to the justness of their own personal position, and the mechanisms through which this position has been attained. That workers be resigned to their position in production is perhaps adequate; that they be reconciled is even preferable.

The contribution of IQ-ism to the legitimation of these social relations is based on a view of society that asserts the efficiency and technological necessity of modern industrial organization, and is buttressed by evidence of the similarity of production and work in such otherwise divergent social systems as the United States and the Soviet Union. In this view large-scale production is a requirement of advanced technology, and the hierarchical division of labor is the only effective means of coordinating the highly complex and interdependent parts of the large-scale productive system. Thus bureaucratic order is awarded the status of an "evolutionary universal"; in the words of Talcott Parsons: "Bureaucracy . . . is the most effective large-scale administrative organization that man has invented, and there is no direct substitute for it."[39]

The hallmark of the "technocratic perspective" is its reduction of a complex web of social relations in production to a few rules of technological efficacy—whence its easy integration with the similarly technocratic view of social stratification inherent in the IQ ideology. In this view the hierarchical division of labor arises from its natural superiority in the coordination of collective activity

39. Talcott Parsons, "Evolutionary Universals in Society," *American Sociological Review* 29, no. 3 (June 1964): 507.

and in the nurturing of expertise in the control of complex production processes. In order to motivate the most
able individuals to undertake the necessary training and
preparation for high level occupational roles, salaries and
status must be closely associated with one's level in the
work hierarchy. Thus Davis and Moore, in their highly
influential "functional theory of stratification," locate the
"determinants of differential reward" in "differential
functional importance" and "differential scarcity of personnel." "Social inequality," they conclude, "is thus an
unconsciously evolved device by which societies insure
that the most important positions are conscientiously
filled by the most qualified persons."[40] Herrnstein is a
little more concrete: "If virtually anyone is smart enough
to be a ditch digger, and only half the people are smart
enough to be engineers, then society is, in effect, husbanding its intellectual resources by holding engineers in
greater esteem and paying them more."[41]

This perspective, technocratic in its justification of the
hierarchical division of labor, leads smoothly to a meritocratic view of the process of matching individuals to jobs.
An efficient and impersonal bureaucracy assesses the individual purely in terms of his or her expected contribution to production. The main determinants of an individual's expected job fitness are seen as those cognitive
and psycho-motor capacities relevant to the worker's
technical ability to do the job. The technocratic view of
production and the meritocratic view of job allocation
yield an important corollary, to which we will later return.
Namely, there is always a strong tendency in an efficient
industrial order to abjure caste, class, sex, color, and
ethnic origins in occupational placement. This tendency

40. K. Davis and W. E. Moore, "Some Principles of Stratification," in *Class, Status and Power*, eds. Reinhard Bendix and Sey-
mour M. Lipset (New York: Free Press, 1966).

41. Herrnstein, "IQ," p. 51.

will be particularly strong in a capitalist economy, where competitive pressures constrain employers to hire on the basis of strict efficiency criteria.[42]

The technocratic view of production, along with the meritocratic view of hiring, provides the strongest form of legitimation of work organization and social stratification in capitalist society. Not only is the notion that the hierarchical division of labor is "technically necessary" (albeit politically totalitarian) strongly reinforced, but also the view that job allocation is just and egalitarian (albeit severely unequal) is ultimately justified as objective, efficient, and necessary. Moreover, the individual's reconciliation with his or her own position in the hierarchy of production appears all but complete: the legitimacy of the authority of superiors no less than that of the individual's own objective position flows not from social contrivance but from science and reason.

That this view does not strain the credulity of well-paid intellectuals is perhaps not surprising.[43] Nor would the technocratic/meritocratic perspective be of much use in legitimizing the hierarchical division of labor were its adherents to be counted only among the university elite and the technical and professional experts. But such is not the case. Despite the extensive evidence that IQ is not an important determinant of individual occupational achievement (Section 2), and despite the fact that few occupations place cognitive requirements on job entry, the crucial importance of IQ in personal success has captured the public mind. Numerous attitude surveys exhibit this fact. In a national sample of high school students, for example, "intelligence" ranks second only to "good

42. For a statement of this position, see Milton Friedman, *Capitalism and Freedom* (Chicago: University of Chicago Press, 1962).

43. Jensen reports that a panel of "experts" determined that higher status jobs "require" higher IQ. See Jensen, "How Much Can We Boost IQ."

health" in importance as a desirable personal attribute.[44]
Similarly a large majority chose "intelligence" along with
"hard work" as the most important requirements of success in life. The public concern over the Coleman Report
findings about scholastic achievement and the furor over
the IQ debate are merely indications of the pervasiveness
of the IQ ideology.

This popular acceptance, we shall argue, is due to the
unique role of the educational system.

Education and Legitimation

To understand the widespread acceptance of the view
that economic success is predicated on intellectual
achievement we must look beyond the workplace, for the
IQ ideology does not conform to most workers' everyday
experience on the job. Rather, the strength of this view
derives in large measure from the interaction between
schooling, cognitive achievement, and economic success.
IQ-ism legitimates the hierarchical division of labor not
directly, but primarily through its relationship with the
educational system.

We can summarize the relationship as follows. First,
the distribution of rewards by the school is seen as being
based on objectively measured cognitive achievement
and is therefore fair.* Second, schools are seen as being

---

*Recent studies, such as Hanser, Heyns, and Jencks, indeed
indicate a lack of social class or racial bias in school grades: given
a student's cognitive attainment, his or her grades seem not to
be significantly affected by class or racial origins, at least on the
high school level. See Robert Hauser, "Schools and the Stratification Process," *American Journal of Sociology*, 74 (May 1969):
587–611; Barbara Heyns, "Curriculum Assignment and Tracking Policies in Forty-Eight Urban Public High Schools" (Ph.D.
diss., University of Chicago, 1971); Jencks, *Inequality*. On the

44. O. G. Brim et al., *American Beliefs and Attitudes about Intelligence* (New York: Russell Sage Foundation, 1969).

primarily oriented toward the production of cognitive skills. Third, higher levels of schooling are seen as a major, perhaps the strongest, determinant of economic success, and quite reasonably so, given the strong association of these two variables exhibited in Table 2. It is concluded, thus, that high IQs are acquired in a fair and open competition in school and in addition are a major determinant of success. The conclusion is based on the belief that the relationship between level of schooling and degree of economic success derives largely from the contribution of school to an individual's cognitive skills. Given the organization and stated objectives of schools it is easy to see how people would come to accept this belief. We have shown in Tables 2 and 5 that it is largely without empirical support.

The linking of intelligence to economic success indirectly via the educational system strengthens rather than weakens the legitimation process. First, the day-to-day contact of parents and children with the competitive, cognitively oriented school environment, with clear connections to the economy, buttresses in a very immediate and concrete way the technocratic perspective on economic organization, to a degree that a sporadic and impersonal testing process divorced from the school environment could not aspire. Second, by rendering the outcome (educational attainment) dependent not only on ability but also on motivation, drive to achieve, perseverance, and sacrifice, the status allocation mechanism acquires heightened legitimacy. Moreover, personal attributes are tested and developed over a long period of time, thus enhancing the apparent objectivity and achievement

---

other hand, school grades are by no means based on cognitive achievement alone. An array of behavior and personality traits are rewarded as well—particularly those relevant to the student's future participation in the production system. For a statistical treatment of this question, see Gintis, "Education and the Characteristics of Worker Productivity."

orientation of the stratification system. Third, by gradually "cooling out" individuals at different educational levels, the student's aspirations are relatively painlessly brought into line with his probable occupational status. By the time most students terminate schooling they have validated for themselves their inability or unwillingness to be a success at the next highest level. Through competition, success, and defeat in the classroom, the individual is reconciled to his or her social position.[45]

The statistical results of the previous section fit in well with our description of the role of education in the legitimation process. The IQ ideology better legitimates the hierarchical division of labor the stronger are the statistical associations of IQ with level of schooling and economic success, and the weaker are the causal relations.* Weak causal relationships are also necessary for the efficient operation of the job allocation process. IQ is in fact *not* a crucial determinant of job adequacy; the placement of workers solely, or even largely, on the basis of cognitive abilities would seriously inhibit the efficient allocation of workers to occupational slots. Thus there must be a strong statistical association of IQ with economic success, but little economic reward for having a higher IQ in the absence of other traits normally associated with high IQ.[46] Similarly there must be a strong statistical association between IQ and school success (grades), but enough individual variation to render "hard work" or good

---

*By "statistical association" we refer to the simple correlation coefficient between the two variables. By "causal relation" we mean the partial derivative of one variable with respect to another, namely, the effect of a change in one variable on another, holding constant all other relevant variables.

45. See Burton R. Clark, "The 'Cooling Out' Function in Higher Education," *American Journal of Sociology* 65, no. 6 (May 1960); Paul Lauter and Florence Howe, "The Schools Are Rigged for Failure," *New York Review of Books*, June 20, 1970.
46. See Tables 1 and 4.

behavior important.[47] Again there must be a strong statistical association between school success and final level
of education attainment, but enough individual variation
to allow any "sufficiently motivated" student to achieve
higher educational levels. Lastly there must be a strong
association between level of education and economic success, but enough individual variation to reward "achievement motivation" and to allow for the multitude of personal attributes of differential value in educational and
occupational performance.[48] All of these conditions appear to be satisfied.

The History of Legitimation: IQ, Education, and Eugenics

The relationship between schooling, IQ and the stratification system is therefore by no means technologically
determined within the framework of capitalist economic
institutions. Nor did it arise accidentally. Rather, a growing body of historical research indicates that it grew out
of a more or less conscious and coordinated attempt to
generate a disciplined industrial labor force and to legitimate the rapid hierarchization of the division of labor
around the turn of the century.[49]

This research strongly contests the dominant "liberal-
technocratic" analysis of education. This "technocratic"
view of schooling, economic success, and the requisites

47. See Gintis, "Education and Characteristics of Worker Productivity"; Edwards, "Alienation and Inequality."
48. See Bowles, "Unequal Education and the Reproduction of
the Social Division of Labor."
49. For an extensive bibliography of this research, see Herbert
Gintis, "Toward a Political Economy of Education: A Radical
Critique of Ivan Illich's *Deschooling Society,*" *Harvard Educational
Review* 42, no. 1 (February 1972); Bowles, "Unequal Education
and the Reproduction of the Social Division of Labor"; Colin
Greer, *The Great School Legend* (New York: Basic Books, 1972).

of job functioning supplies an elegant and logically coherent (if not empirically accurate) explanation of the
historical rise of mass education in the process of industrial development. Because modern industry, irrespective
of its political and institutional framework, consists in the
application of increasingly complex and cognitively de-
manding operational technologies, these cognitive demands require an increasing level of cognitive competence on the part of the labor force as a whole. Thus the
expansion of educational opportunity becomes a requi-
site of modern economic growth.[50] Formal education, by
extending to the masses what had been throughout history the privilege of the few, opens the superior levels in
the production hierarchy to all with the ability and willingness to attain such competencies. Hence the observed
association between education and economic success reflects the achievement of a fundamentally egalitarian
school system in promoting cognitive development.

Quite apart from the erroneous view that the determinants of job adequacy in modern industry are primarily
cognitive, this interpretation of the rise of universal education in the United States finds little support in the historical record. Mass education made its beginning in cit-
ies and towns where the dominant industries required
little skill—and far less cognitive ability—among the work
force. The towns in which the skill-using industries
located were the followers, not the leaders, in the process

---

50. See Frank Tracy Carleton, *Economic Influences upon Educational Progress in the U.S., 1820–1850* (Madison, Wis.: University
of Wisconsin Press, 1908); Theodore W. Schultz, "Capital For-
mation by Education," *Journal of Political Economics* 68 (December
1960): 571–583. This ideology is discussed in its several varia-
tions in Samuel Bowles and Herbert Gintis, "The Ideology of
Progressive School Reform," in *Work, Technology, and Education:
Essays in the Intellectual Foundations of Education*, eds. Henry Rose-
mont and Walter Feinberg (Urbana: University of Illinois Press,
forthcoming), and Greer, *The Great School Legend*.

of mid-nineteenth-century educational reform and expansion.[51] Likewise in the late nineteenth-century rural
West and South the expansion of schooling was associated, not with the application of modern technology
or mechanization to farming, but with the extension of
the wage labor system to agricultural employment.[52]
Even the rise of the land-grant colleges—those institutions that in the popular wisdom were most finely attuned
to producing the technical skills required in the modernizing agricultural sectors—cannot be explained by the
cognitive needs of the economy, for during their first
thirty or so years of operation they offered hardly any
instruction in agricultural sciences.[53]

Thus the growth of the modern educational system did
not originate with the rising cognitive requirements of
the economy. Rather, the birth and early development of
universal education was sparked by the critical need of a
burgeoning capitalist order for a stable work force and
citizenry reconciled, if not inured, to the wage labor system. Order, docility, discipline, sobriety, and humility—

51. See David Bruck, "The Schools of Lowell" (honors thesis,
Harvard University, 1971). In his study of cotton mill workers in
Lowell in the 1840s, Hal Luft ("The Industrial Worker in Lowell," unpublished manuscript, Harvard University, 1972) revealed no relationship whatever between worker literacy and
their physical productivity. Bowles's as yet unpublished study
(jointly with Alexander Field) of nineteenth-century educational
expansion in Massachusetts found that the leading towns were
those with cotton industries and large concentrations of foreign-
born workers.

52. This is the conclusion of Robert Muchele and James
Medoff ("Education and the Agrarian Order," unpublished
manuscript, Harvard University, January 1972) based on a statistical study of U.S. census data. Their study sharply contradicts
the interpretation of Douglass North in *The Economic Growth of the
U.S., 1790–1860* (New York, 1961).

53. See William Lazonick, "The Integration of Higher Education into Agricultural Production in the U.S." (unpublished
manuscript, Harvard University, 1972).

attributes required by the new social relation of production—were admitted by all concerned as the social benefits of schooling.[54] The popular view of the economy as a technical system would await Frederick Taylor and his scientific management movement; the Social Darwinist emphasis on intelligence appeared only in the "scientific genetics" of Binet and Terman. The integration of the IQ ideology into educational theory and practice had to await basic turn-of-the-century developments in the industrial order itself.

The most important of these developments was the birth of the modern corporation, with its relentless pressure toward uniformity and objectivity in the staffing of ever more finely graded hierarchical positions. The rationalistic efficiency orientation of bureaucratic order was quickly taken over by a growing educational system.[55] Taylorism in the classroom meant competition, hierarchy, uniformity, and, above all, individual accountability by means of objective testing.

A second related source of educational change emanating from the economy was the changing nature of the work force. Work on the family farm or in the artisan shop continued to give way to employment in large-scale enterprises. And millions of immigrants swelled the ranks of the new working class. The un-American, undomesticated character of this transformed work force was quickly revealed in a new labor militancy (of which Sacco and Vanzetti are merely the shadow in folk history) and a skyrocketing public welfare burden.

The accommodation of the educational system to these

54. Bowles, "Unequal Education and the Reproduction of the Social Division of Labor," develops this argument in more detail. This perspective on the use of education is supported by a growing number of historical studies. See Bruck, "The Schools of Lowell," and Katz, *The Irony of Early School Reform.*

55. R. Callahan, *Education and the Cult of Efficiency* (Chicago: University of Chicago Press, 1962).

new economic realities was by no means a placid process.
Modern education was constructed on the rapidly disin-
tegrating and chaotic foundations of the old common
school. Geared to the small town, serving native American Protestant stock, and based on the proliferation of
the one-room schoolhouse, the common school was
scarcely up to supplying the exploding labor needs of the
new corporate order. Dramatic was its failure to deal
effectively with the seething urban agglomeration of
European immigrants of rural and peasant origin.[56] As
large numbers of working-class and particularly immigrant children began attending high schools, the older
democratic ideology of the common school—that the
same curriculum should be offered to all children—gave
way to the "progressive" insistence that education
should be tailored to the "needs of the child."* In the
interests of providing an education relevant to the later
life of the students, vocational schools and tracks were
developed for the children of working families.† The aca-

---

*The superintendent of the Boston schools summed up the
change in 1908:

> Until very recently (the schools) have offered equal oppor-
> tunity for all to receive *one kind* of education, but what will
> make them democratic is to provide opportunity for all to
> receive such education as will fit them *equally well* for their
> particular life work.

In Boston, Documents of the School Committee, 1908, #7, p.
53, quoted in David K. Cohen and Marvin Lazerson, "Education
and the Corporate Order," *Socialist Revolution* (March 1972).

† Sol Cohens "The Industrial Education Movement, 1906–
1917," *American Quarterly,* 20 (Spring 1970) describes this process. Typical of the arguments then given for vocational education is the following, by the superintendent of schools in
Cleveland:

> It is obvious that the educational needs of children in a
> district where the streets are well paved and clean, where

56. See Marvin Lazerson, *Origins of the Urban School* (Cambridge: Harvard University Press, 1971).

demic curriculum was preserved for those who would later have the opportunity to make use of book learning either in college or in white-collar employment.

The frankness with which students were channeled into curriculum tracks on the basis of their race, ethnicity, or social class background raised serious doubts concerning the "openness" of the social class structure. The relation between social class and a child's chances of promotion or tracking assignments was disguised—though not mitigated much—by another "progressive" reform: "objective" educational testing. Particularly after World War I the increased use of intelligence and scholastic achievement testing offered an ostensibly unbiased means of measuring the product of schooling and stratifying students.[57] The complementary growth of the guidance counseling profession allowed much of the channeling to proceed from the students' own well counseled choices, thus adding an apparent element of voluntarism to the system.

If the rhetoric of the educational response to the economic changes after the turn of the century was "progressive," much of its content and consciousness was sup-

---

the homes are spacious and surrounded by lawns and trees, where the language of the child's playfellows is pure, and where life in general is permeated with the spirit and ideals of America—it is obvious that the educational needs of such a child are radically different from those of the child who lives in a foreign and tenement section.

In William H. Elson and Frank P. Bachman, "Different Course for Elementary School," *Educational Review,* 39 (April 1910). See also Lawrence Cremin, *The Transformation of the School* (New York: Alfred A. Knopf, 1964); and Cohen and Lazerson, "Education and the Corporate Order."

57. See Callahan, *Education and the Cult of Efficiency;* David K. Cohen and Marvin Lazerson, "Education and the Corporate Order," *Socialist Revolution* (March 1972); and Lawrence Cremin, *The Transformation of the School* (New York: Alfred A. Knopf, 1964).

plied by the new science of "evolutionary genetics," in the form of the prestigious and influential Eugenics Movement.[58] Of course, as Karier notes, "the nativism, racism, elitism, and social class bias which were so much a part of the testing and Eugenics Movement in America were, in a broader sense, part of the *Zeitgeist* which was America." Yet its solid grounding in Mendel's Law, Darwin, and the sophisticated statistical methodologies of Pearson, Thurstone, and Thorndike lent it the air of scientific rigor previously accorded only to the Newtonian sciences.

The leitmotiv of the testing movement was the uniting constitutional character of human excellence, as rooted in genetic endowment. Moral character, intelligence, and social worth were inextricably connected and biologically rooted. In the words of the eminent psychologist Edward L. Thorndike, "to him that a superior intellect is given has also on the average a superior character."[59] A glance at the new immigrant communities, the black rural ghettos, and the "breeding" of the upper classes could not but confirm this opinion in the popular mind. Statistical information came quickly from that architect of the still popular Stanford-Binet intelligence test—Lewis M. Terman—who confirmed the association of IQ and occupational status. Study after study, moreover, exhibited the low intelligence of "wards of the state" and social deviants.

That a school system geared toward moral development and toward domesticating a labor force for the rising corporate order might readily embrace standardization and testing—to the benefit of the leaders as well as

58. For a short review of this movement and its relation to the development of the United States stratification system, see Karier, "Testing for Order and Control in the Corporate Liberal State."

59. Edward C. Thorndike, "Intelligence and Its Uses," *Harper's*, 140 (January 1920).

the led—goes without saying. Thus it is not surprising that, while the idealistic Progressives worked in vain for a humanistic, more egalitarian education,[60] the bureaucratization and test orientation of the school system proceeded smoothly, well-oiled by seed money from the Carnegie Corporation and other large private foundations, articulated by social scientists at prestigious schools of education[61] and readily implemented by business-controlled local school boards.[62]

The success of the "cult of efficiency" in education, while obviously secured through the political power of private and public corporate elites, would have appeared unthinkable outside the framework of a burgeoning corporate order within which the "system problem" of a stable labor force demanded new and creative institutional mechanisms. Only a strong labor movement dedicated to construction of a qualitatively different social order could have prevented this, or a functionally equivalent, outcome.

We conclude that the present relation of schooling, IQ, and economic success originated quite consciously as part of an attempt to administer and legitimate a new economic order based on the hierarchical division of labor. We reject the notion that the school system does or has ever functioned primarily to produce cognitive skills made scarce and hence valuable by the continuing modernization of the economy.

Our analysis of the contemporary structure of labor rewards, as well as our historical analysis, suggests that cognitive ability is not a particularly scarce good, and

60. Cremin, *The Transformation of the School.*

61. Karier, "Testing for Order and Control in the Corporate Liberal State."

62. George S. Counts, "The Social Composition of Boards of Education," *Review and Elementary School Journal,* Supplementary Education Monographs, no. 33 (1927); Callahan, *Education and the Cult of Efficiency.*

hence bears little independent reward. This conclusion will hardly be news to employers: a cotton manufacturer wrote to Horace Mann, then Secretary of the Massachusetts Board of Education, in 1841:

> I have never considered mere knowledge . . . as the only advantage derived from a good Common School education. . . . (Workers with more education possess) a higher and better state of morals, are more orderly and respectful in their deportment, and more ready to comply with the wholesome and necessary regulations of an establishment. . . . In times of agitation, on account of some change in regulations or wages, I have always looked to the most intelligent, best educated and the most moral for support. The ignorant and uneducated I have generally found the most turbulent and troublesome, acting under the impulse of excited passion and jealousy.[63]

Adequate cognitive skills, we conclude, are generated as a by-product of the current structure of family life and schooling. This highly functional mechanism for the production and stratification of labor has acquired its present form in the pursuit of objectives quite remote from the production of intellectual skills. We turn now to a more searching consideration of its workings.

5. THE REPRODUCTION OF THE HIERARCHICAL DIVISION OF LABOR

A Preview

We have argued that IQ plays an important role in legitimating the stratification system, but that individual differences in IQ are not an important source of differences in levels of economic success. What, then, does determine an individual's chances of rising to the top? Why is it that economically successful parents tend to have economi-

63. Quoted in Katz, *The Irony of Early School Reform*, p. 88.

cally successful children? In this section we seek to explain how social class background interacts with schooling to influence an individual's chances of economic success and in so doing to reproduce a family's position in the hierarchical division of labor.

The argument may be briefly summarized at the outset. To get a job at any particular level in the hierarchy of production one has to meet two tests: first, one must be able and willing to do the work; and second, one must be of appropriate race, sex, age, education, and demeanor so that his or her assignment to the job will contribute to the sense that the social order of the firm is just. Thus criteria of worker adequacy reflect more than the employer's desire that workers be hardworking and capable. They reflect as well the need for acquiescence to the employer's monopolization of power. Thus the perpetuation and legitimation of the hierarchical division of labor within the enterprise is an important additional objective of employers in the selection and placement of workers. The smooth exercise of control from the top of the enterprise rests on the daily reconfirmation of the employee's sense of the just claim of his or her superiors, coworkers, and subordinates to their particular jobs.

The ability to operate well at a particular level in the hierarchy and the legitimate claim to one's place in the authority structure and to the rewards associated with it depend to a large extent on experiences in the home and at school. The enterprise is by no means a full-blown socialization agency capable of shaping worker consciousness and behavior to its needs; its control over recruitment and internal organization can but *reinforce* patterns of consciousness developed in the larger society. That is, the particular structure of authority within the firm that will be seen as legitimate—whether based on distinctions of race, sex, educational credentials, age, manners of speech, or whatever—is an expression of broader social values and prejudices. And these too are both reflected in and dependent upon the structure of family life and schooling. Specifically we argue that a work force that is both competent to do the job and consistent with the perpetuation of the hierarchical division of labor is generated in large measure through a correspondence between the social relations of production, on the one hand, and the social relations of schooling and of family life, on the other. At the same time the corresponding relations of family life, schooling, and work tend to reproduce economic status differences among families from generation to generation.

The Criteria of Hireability

We begin with an obvious point: in capitalist society the income and social position of the vast majority of individuals derive predominately from the sale of their labor services to employers. An adequate explanation of the stratification process thus requires understanding (1) the criteria used by employers in hiring, tenure, promotion, and pay; (2) the processes whereby these criteria come to be seen as fair and legitimate; and (3) the process whereby individuals come to acquire those attributes relevant to employers' criteria.

The *prima facie* dimensions of job-relevant individual attributes are vast indeed. They include (at least) such features as ownership of physical implements (e.g., the medieval knight owned his horse, armor, and retinue), membership (e.g., the feudal guild master), ascription (e.g., sex, race, social class, age, caste, religion), and personal attributes (e.g., skills, motivation, attitudes, personality, credentials). In capitalist society it is the last of these along with a few important ascriptive traits—sex, race, and age—that come to the fore. Indeed even the relationship between social class background and economic success operates in large measure through differences in personal characteristics associated with differential family status. Employers never ask about social background.*

Thus our inquiry into the stratification process must focus on the supply, demand, and production of those personal attributes and ascriptive traits that are relevant to getting ahead in the world of work. We may begin with the demand for personal attributes by employers. While employers may have certain restrictions in their hiring practices (child labor and antidiscrimination laws, union regulations, social pressures), by and large their sole objective in hiring is to insure the ability of individuals to perform adequately in the work role in question. The requirements of job adequacy in any job, of course, depend on the entire structure of work roles, that is, on the social relations of production within the enterprise. Thus we must first inquire into the criteria by which work is organized. What determines the structure of work roles —in capitalist society characterized by hierarchy, job fragmentation, bureaucracy, and control from the top of the organization?

One objective of capitalists—both as a class and as individuals—is to perpetuate their class standing. Thus work roles must be organized so as to reproduce the position of capitalists and allied high level management in the social relations of production. A closely related second objective is securing adequate long-term profits, without which the enterprise would cease to exist. Thus profits are sought both as an instrument in maintaining the class status of the directors of the firm

---

*Warner et al., in their extensive empirical studies of stratification, place much emphasis on social class ascription. See W. Lloyd Warner et al., *Who Shall Be Educated?* (New York: Harper, 1944). Compare Warner and Paul S. Lunt, *The Social Life of a Modern Community* (New Haven, Conn.: Yale University Press, 1941). But this seems characteristic only of the "smalltown" economic community, rapidly becoming past history.

and as their major source of income.*

In the joint pursuit of profits and the perpetuation of their class standing, the directors of an enterprise seek to meet three immediate objectives—sometimes complementary, sometimes in conflict: technical efficiency, control, and legitimacy. Technical efficiency requires that the structure of work roles be organized so that for a given set of inputs—labor, raw materials, equipment, etc.—the maximum possible output will be produced. The second objective, control over the production process, requires both the retention of decision-making power at the top and the maintenance of labor costs in line with those prevailing in the economy as a whole. Both forms of control are highly problematic. First, as we have emphasized, the political organization of the enterprise is totalitarian, while the external political process is formally democratic. Where possible, workers demand control over the decision making about working conditions toward the improvement of their condition. Organizing production hierarchically and fragmenting tasks, by dividing workers on different levels against one another and reducing the independent range of control of each, both weaken the solidarity (and hence limit the group power) of workers and serve to convince them, through their day-to-day activities, of their personal incapacity to control—and even of its technical infeasibility. Thus hiring criteria and the structuring of work roles are based on

*Indeed under conditions of perfect competition the maximization of profits is a necessary condition for the reproduction of the capitalists' class position. We need not here enter into the complicated debate on whether firms do indeed seek to maximize profits. For a survey see Edwards, "Alienation and Inequality." We conclude that the relevant behavioral implication of the theories that posit other objectives (sales or employment maximization, for example) are; in the context of the by and large competitive milieu of the United States economy, virtually indistinguishable from those of profit maximization.

the principle of "divide and conquer."[64] That the satisfaction of this control objective often conflicts with technical efficiency is illustrated by the many studies documenting significant increases in productivity and worker
satisfaction associated with shifts toward worker participation in decision making, greater job breadth, and the
use of work teams.[65] But efficiency and profitability are,
of course, different things.

A third objective is that work roles be organized so as
to legitimize the authority relations in the firm. That is,
relations among superiors, subordinates, and peers must
not violate the norms of the larger society, and the right
of the superior to direct as well as the duty of the subordinate to submit must draw on general cultural values. It is
for this reason that a superior must always have a higher
salary than a subordinate, whatever the conditions of
relative supply of the two types of labor. It is also for this
reason that in a racist and sexist society blacks and
women cannot in general be placed above whites or men
in the line of hierarchical authority. Employers ordinarily
structure work roles so that young people will not boss
older people. In terms of personal attributes, modes of
self-presentation are also important; however well they
actually function technically, individuals must seem fit for
their position and must actively protect their prerogatives
and the structure of work roles (especially their own).[66]
Educational *credentials* enter here as well: it is desirable to
associate hierarchical authority with level of education,

64. See Marglin, "What Do Bosses Do?"

65. For reviews of the evidence, see Blumberg, *Industrial
Democracy;* Victor H. Vroom, "Industrial Social Psychology," in
The Handbook of Social Psychology, eds. G. Lindsey and E. Aaronsen
(Reading, Mass.: Addison-Wesley, 1969); Gintis, "Power and
Alienation"; and Andre Gorz, *Strategy for Labor* (Boston: Beacon
Press, 1968).

66. For more on this, see Erving Goffman, *The Presentation of
Self in Everyday Life* (New York: Doubleday, 1959).

not only because higher levels of schooling may enable an employee to better do the work at hand or because the more educated seem more fit by their demeanor to hold authority, but also simply because educational achievement, as symbolized by one sort of sheepskin or another, legitimates authority according to prevailing social values. Indeed this fact lies at the root of the IQ ideology described above.

From this analysis of the capitalist objectives governing the organization of work roles in the enterprise, we may derive some insight into the employers' demand for particular worker attributes. Our analysis suggests five important sets of worker characteristics. First, we have noted the emphasis of the "technocratic perspective" on cognitive attributes—such as scholastic achievement—to which we may add concrete technical and operational skills (e.g., knowing how to do typing, accounting, chemical engineering, or carpentry). Second, there are, parallel to cognitive attributes, a set of personality traits (such as motivation, perseverance, docility, dominance, flexibility, or tact) that enable the individual to operate effectively in a work role. Third, there are traits that we may call modes of self-presentation[67] such as manner of speech and dress, patterns of peer identification, and perceived "social distance" from individuals and groups of different social position. These traits do not necessarily contribute to the worker's execution of tasks, but may be valuable to employers in their effort to stabilize, validate, and legitimize the particular structure of work roles in the organization as a whole. Similar in function are our fourth set of traits: ascriptive characteristics such as race, sex, and age. Finally we may add to our list of attributes credentials, such as level and prestige of education, which, like modes of self-presentation and the ascriptive traits, are a resource used by employers to add

67. See ibid. for a more thorough analysis.

to the overall legitimacy of the organization.

The analytical problem, of course, is to determine the precise content of these five factors, and how each affects the stratification process. This problem is particularly difficult in that all five tend to occur together in a single individual. Thus an individual with more cognitive achievement and skills will also, on the average, be more capable personality-wise of operating on higher occupational levels, will speak, dress, and exhibit a pattern of loyalties befitting the corresponding social class, and will have proper credentials to boot (though she may be a woman!). But since there is still a great deal of variation among individuals in their relative possession of these various attributes, analysis is not impossible. Indeed a major statistically supported assertion of this essay is that cognitive attributes are not central to the determination of social stratification, and hence the association of cognitive level and access to higher level occupations must be largely a by-product of selection on the basis of others.

We believe that all four of the remaining types of personal attributes—personality traits relevant to the work task, modes of self-presentation, ascriptive traits, and credentials—are integral to the stratification process. Indeed we shall argue that all four are systematically used by employers to affect the reproduction of the hierarchical division of labor, and, as such, their importance in the determination of economic success is not an expression of irrational and uninformed employment policies, subject to correction by "enlightened" employment practices and social legislation. Instead, we shall argue in our concluding section that the link between the social relations of production and the stratification process is so intimate that any qualitative change in the latter is contingent upon the transformation of the hierarchical division of labor as the archetype of productive activity.*

*We would like to show further that the hierarchical division

We do not yet understand precisely how these four noncognitive types of worker traits interact, or the extent to which each contributes to the stratification process. The strong association between education and economic success, plus the relative unimportance of cognitive achievement as a criterion of job placement, nevertheless convinces us of their overall decisive impact. We shall present evidence for the importance of each in turn, beginning with the job-relevant personality traits.

The personality traits required of "efficient" workers must correspond by and large to the requirements of harmonious integration into the bureaucratic order of the enterprise. This order exhibits four essential characteristics. First, the duties, responsibilities, and privileges of individuals are determined neither according to individual preference nor flexible cooperative decision by workers, but rather by a system of rules that precedes the individual's participation and sets limits on his or her actions. Second, the relations among individuals are characterized, according to the rules of the organization, by hierarchical authority and interdependence. An individual's actions are closely tied to the wills of his or her superiors, and the results of his or her actions have repercussions on large numbers of other workers. Third, while control from the top is manifested in rules, the principle of hierarchical authority implies that large numbers of workers have essential, though circumscribed, areas of

---

of labor, far from flowing naturally from the exigencies of productive efficiency, has taken its present form in response to the continuous struggles of capitalists for hegemony in the control of economic activity. From this perspective the stratification system can be seen as the product of the class struggle between capitalists and workers. Given our present understanding of these issues, however, no brief survey of the evidence could do justice to the argument, to which we hope to return in a later paper. For extended historical and contemporary treatments that we find persuasive, see Marglin, "What Do Bosses Do?" and Edwards, "Alienation and Inequality."

decision and choice. Fourth, the formal nature of the organization and the fact that work roles are determined on the basis of profitability and compatibility with control from the apex of the pyramidal organization imply that workers cannot be adequately motivated by the intrinsic rewards of the work process.[68]

These characteristics of the hierarchical division of labor determine the personality traits required of workers. Some of these are general traits valuable to the employer at all levels of hierarchy and status. All workers must be dependable (i.e., follow rules) because of the strong emphasis on rules and the complex interrelations among tasks that define the enterprise. Similarly all workers must be properly subordinate to authority—diligent in carrying out orders as opposed to merely obeying rules. Further all workers, insofar as they have areas of personal initiative and choice, must internalize the values of the organization, using its criteria as a basis for decision. Lastly all workers must respond adequately to the external incentives of the organization—the crudest being threat of dismissal, and the more subtle including the possibility of promotion to higher status, authority, or pay. Thus the worker must work equally efficiently independent from personal feelings about the particular task at hand.

While these requirements hold for all workers, there are important qualitative differences among levels. These tend to follow directly from differences in the scope of independent decision making, which increases with hierarchical status. Thus the lowest level of worker must simply refrain from breaking rules. On the highest level it becomes crucial that the worker internalize the values of the organization, act out of personal initiative, and know when not to go by the book. In between, workers must be

68. See Herbert Gintis, "New Working Class and Revolutionary Youth," *Socialist Revolution*, May 1970.

methodical, predictable, and persevering, and at a somewhat higher level, must respond flexibly to their superiors, whose directives acquire a complexity transcending
the relatively few rules that apply directly to their tasks.
Thus we would expect the crucial determinants of job
adequacy to pass from rule following to dependability-
predictability to subordinateness to internalized values,
all with an overlap of motivation according to external
incentives and penalties (doubtless with penalties playing
a larger role at the lower levels, and incentives at the
higher).

Much of this description of functional personal attributes of job performance is based on the work of Richard
Edwards, and has been supported by his empirical research.[69] Edwards argues that supervisor ratings of employees—as the basic determinant of hirings, firings, and
promotions—are the best measure of job adequacy and
are the implements of the organization's stratification
mechanism. Thus Edwards compared supervisor ratings
on these workers with a set of thirty-two personality ratings by the workers' peers. In a large sample of Boston-
area workers, he finds that a cluster of three personality
traits—which he summarizes as respect for rules, dependability, and internalization of the norms of the firm—
predicts strongly* supervisor ratings of workers in the
same work group, while such attributes as age, sex, social
class background, education, and intelligence have little
additional predictive value. In addition, Edwards noted
that respect for rules was most important at the lower
occupational levels, dependability appearing strongly for
middle levels, and internalization of the norms of the firm
predicting best at the higher levels.

When we pass to the literature documenting the im-

*$R^2 = 38$ percent, uncorrected for errors in measurement and
reliability.

69. See Edwards, "Alienation and Inequality."

portance of self-presentation as attributes relevant to the allocation of individuals to status positions, we are faced with a difficult problem of assessment. Numerous studies have shown these personal attributes to be definite (albeit often covert) criteria for hiring and promotion.[70] Being descriptive and analytical rather than statistical, however, they defy comparison with other data on personal attributes as to importance in the stratification process. We must content ourselves with a simple presentation of the arguments.

"A status," says Goffman, " . . . is not a material thing; it is a pattern of appropriate conduct, coherent, embellished, and well articulated."[71] That is, apart from the "reality" of task performance, role fulfillment requires the "contrivance" of legitimation—legitimation of the role itself as well as the individual's personal right to fill it. Thus the doctor not only must cure but also must exude the aura of infallibility and dedication fitting for one whose critical acts intervene between life and death. Similarly, the supervisor not only must supervise but also must exhibit his inevitable distance from and superiority to his inferiors, and his ideal suitability for his position. Thus role fulfillment requires a dramatic "theatrical" performance—an impulse toward idealization of role—on a routinized and internalized basis. Goffman documents the importance of self-presentation in a vast array of social positions—those of doctors, nurses, waitresses, dentists, military personnel, mental patients, funeral directors, eighteenth-century noblemen, Indian castes, Chinese mandarins, junk peddlers, unionized workers, teachers, pharmacists, as well as in the relations between

70. We know of two major presentations, reviews, and overall interpretations of these studies: Goffman, *The Presentation of Self in Everyday Life*, and Claus Offe, *Leistungsprinzip und Industrielle Arbeit* (Frankfort: Europaische Verlaganstalt, 1970).

71. Goffman, *The Presentation of Self in Everyday Life*, p. 75.

men and women and blacks and whites.[72]

Central to Goffman's analysis of self-presentation is his concept of the "front" of a performance, defined as "that part of the individual's performance which regularly functions in a general and fixed fashion to define the situation for those who view the performance."[73] This front consists of personal behavior ("insignia of office or rank; clothing, sex, age, and racial characteristics; size and looks; posture; speech patterns; facial expressions; bodily gestures; and the like") as well as physical setting. Moreover, argues Goffman, these fronts are not merely personal and idiosyncratic, but are socially regularized and channeled, so there is "a tendency for a large number of different acts to be presented behind a small number of fronts."[74] Thus, on the one hand, "modes of self-presentation" take on a social class character, and, on the other, physical settings are allocated not to individuals but to hierarchical levels.

The role of self-presentation in social stratification arises from a similar social treatment of "personal fronts." Social class differences in family and childhood socialization, as well as the informal organization of peer groups along social class lines,[75] are likely to reinforce

72. Other studies may be cited. Gorz ("Capitalist Relations of Production and the Socially Necessary Labor Force") provides a cogent analysis of the self-presentation of technical workers. Offe's analysis (Leistungsprinzip und Industrielle Arbeit) includes evidence on the role of schools in codifying modes of self-presentation and reviews sociological studies of self-presentation and promotability. Finally Bensman and Rosenberg analyze the importance of conscious manipulation of self-presentation among the upwardly mobile. See Joseph Bensman and Bernard Rosenberg, "The Meaning of Work in Bureaucratic Society," in Anxiety and Identity, eds. Maurice Stein et al. (New York: Free Press, 1960).

73. Goffman, The Presentation of Self in Everyday Life, p. 22.

74. Ibid., p. 26.

75. Norman C. Alexander and Ernest Q. Campbell, "Peer Influences on Adolescent Educational Aspirations and Attainments," American Sociological Review 29 (August 1964): 568–575;

social class lines from generation to generation by providing stable reproduction of modes of self-presentation. Similarly social class differences in levels of schooling are likely to develop career identities, symbols and idelogies, organization loyalties, and aspirations apposite to particular levels in the hierarchy of production.

But does self-presentation play a role akin to I Q in the stratification process (i.e., is it by and large a by-product of allocation and socialization mechanisms based on other criteria), or does its importance compare with and perhaps even eclipse job-relevant personality traits? The answer awaits future research.

We may now consider the importance of our last two sets of employability traits: ascriptive characteristics (race, age, sex) and acquired credentials (e.g., educational degrees, seniority). We have argued that the legitimation of the hierarchical division of labor, as well as the smooth day-to-day control over the work process, requires that the authority structure of the enterprise—with its corresponding structure of pay and privilege—respects the wider society's ascriptive and symbolic distinctions. In particular, socially acceptable relations of domination and subordination must be respected: white over black; male over female; old (but not aged) over young; and schooled over unschooled.

We make no claim that these social prejudices origi-

Richard P. Boyle, "On Neighborhood Context and College Plans," *American Sociological Review* 31 (October 1966): 706–707; E. Erickson, "A Study of the Normative Influence of Parents and Friends," in *Self-Concept of Ability and School Achievement,* Wilbur Brookover et al. Cooperative Research Project 2381, Office of Research and Publications, Michigan State University, 1967, vol. 3; A. Haller and C. Butterworth, "Peer Influence on Levels of Occupational and Educational Aspiration," *Social Forces* 38 (May 1960): 289–295; William H. Sewell and Michael Armer, "Neighborhood Context and College Plans," *American Sociological Review* 31 (April 1966): 159–168; Alan Wilson, "Residential Segregation of Social Classes and Aspirations of High School Boys," *American Sociological Review* 24 (December 1959): 836–845.

nated as a capitalist contrivance, although a strong case could probably be made that the form and strength of both sexism and racism here derive in large measure from the particular historical development of capitalist institutions in the United States and Europe. Save credentialist distinctions, all predate the modern capitalist era. "Rational business practice" has reinforced and extended them, while consigning less useful prejudices to the proverbial trash bin of history.* The credentialist mentality, as we have argued, was indeed contrived to perpetuate the concept of social rank in a society increasingly eschewing distinctions of birth.

The individual employer, acting singly, normally takes societal values and beliefs as data, and will violate them only where his long-term financial benefits are secure. The broader prejudices of society are thus used as a resource by bosses in their effort to control labor. In this way the pursuit of profits and security of class position reinforces the racist, sexist, and credentialist mentality. Thus black workers are paid less than whites with equivalent schooling and cognitive achievement,[76] and similarly for women relative to men.[77] Likewise those with more

---

*At the same time, of course, the extension and development of capitalist wage labor tends to destroy class distinctions based on precapitalist social relations of production (such as nepotism, direct social class discrimination in hiring, slave status, caste, and nobility), as these are incompatible with the hierarchical division of labor. Similarly capitalist development is destructive of the ideological underpinnings of all ascriptive norms—even those that are "respected" in the above sense in the day-to-day operation of the enterprise. We shall discuss this contradiction in Section 4.

76. See Randall D. Weiss, "The Effect of Education on the Earnings of Blacks and Whites," *Review of Economics and Statistics* 52 (May 1970); Phillips Cutright, "Achievement, Military Service and Earnings," mimeographed (Cambridge, Mass.: Harvard University, 1969).

77. Marilyn Power Goldberg, "The Economic Exploitation of Women," in *Problems in Political Economy*, ed. David M. Gordon (Lexington, Mass.: D. C. Heath, 1971).

schooling are given preference for supervisory jobs, in the absence of compelling evidence of the superior performance of those less educated.[78] Lastly pay and authority increase over most of a person's working life, out of all proportion to any conceivable on-the-job learning of increased skills.

How Worker Characteristics Are Acquired: The Correspondence Principles

Having surveyed the reasoning and evidence indicating the importance of our four sets of noncognitive worker traits—work-related personality characteristics, modes of self-presentation, ascriptive characteristics, and credentials—we turn now to our last question: how are these determinants of one's place in the stratification system acquired? The ascriptive traits are, of course, acquired at birth, or in the case of age, inescapably as life progresses, so little need be said of them. The acquisition of credentials requires survival in the school system, and is an arduous, but not particularly complex, process. The way in which workers come to have a particular set of work-relevant personality characteristics or modes of self-presentation requires a more searching analysis.

We find the answer to this question in two correspondence principles, which may be stated succinctly as follows: the social relations of schooling and of family life correspond to the social relations of production.

We have suggested above that the social relations of schooling are structured similarly to the social relations of production in several essential respects.[79] The school

78. Ivar Berg, *Education and Jobs: The Great Training Robbery* (New York: Frederick A. Praeger, 1970).

79. For a more extended discussion, see Gintis, "Education and the Characteristics of Worker Productivity"; Gintis, "Toward a Political Economy of Education"; Bowles, "Cuban Edu-

is a bureaucratic order with hierarchical authority, rule orientation, stratification by "ability" (tracking) as well as by age (grades), role differentiation by sex (physical education, home economics, shop), and a system of external incentives (marks, promise of promotion, and threat of failure) much like pay and status in the sphere of work. Thus schools are likely to develop in students traits corresponding to those required on the job. One of us,[80] in a review of the educational literature, has shown that students are graded for personality traits associated with subordinacy, discipline, and rule following quite independently of the level of cognitive achievement. Several studies of vocational training by Gene Smith[81] exhibit the same pattern of reward, and our colleague Peter Meyer[82] has replicated Edwards's results, using the same personality measures, in predicting not "supervision ratings," but "grade point average" in a New York high school. Lastly Edwards's analysis of data on high school records and data work supervision ratings collected by Brenner[83] indicate that variables measuring teacher's evaluation of student conduct are far more important than the student's grade point average in predicting the individual's

cation and the Revolutionary Ideology," *Harvard Educational Review* 41 (November 1971).

80. Gintis, "Education and the Characteristics of Worker Productivity."

81. Gene M. Smith, "Usefulness of Peer Ratings of Personality in Educational Research," *Education and Psychological Measurements* (1967); Smith, "Personality Correlates of Academic Performance in Three Dissimilar Populations," Proceedings of the 77th Annual Convention, American Psychological Association, 1967.

82. Peter J. Meyer, "Schooling and the Reproduction of the Social Division of Labor" (honors thesis, Harvard University, March 1972). See also Edwards, "Alienation and Inequality."

83. Marshall H. Brenner, "Use of High School Data to Predict Work Performance," *Journal of Applied Psychology* 52, no. 1 (January 1968).

work adequacy as perceived by the supervisor.* While more work in this area remains to be done, there are clear indications that the educational system does articulate with the economy in large part via these effective selection and generation mechanisms.

But recall that the work-related personality traits required of employees differ according to the work role in question, those at the base of the hierarchy requiring a heavy emphasis on obedience and rules and those at the top, where the discretionary scope is considerable, requiring a greater ability to make decisions on the basis of well-internalized norms. This pattern is closely replicated in the social relations of schooling. Note the wide range of choice over curriculum, life style, and allocation of time afforded to college students, compared with the obedience and respect for authority expected in high school. Differentiation occurs also within each level of schooling. One needs only to compare the social relations of a junior college with those of an elite four-year college,[84] or those of a working-class high school with those of a wealthy suburban high school, for verification of this point.†

The differential socialization patterns in schools at-

*This is a particularly strong finding in view of the fact that the grades themselves are evidently determined in important measure by the teacher's evaluation of the student's conduct. For a discussion of these data, see Edwards, "Alienation and Inequality."

†Edgar Z. Friedenberg, *Coming of Age in America* (New York: Random House, 1965). It is consistent with this pattern that the play-oriented, child-centered pedagogy of the progressive movement found little acceptance outside of private schools in wealthy communities. See Cohen and Lazerson, "Education and the Corporate Order," and Neil Friedman, "Inequality, Social Control, and the History of Educational Reform" (unpublished manuscript, School of Social Welfare, State University of New York at Stony Brook, 1972).

84. See J. Binstock, *Survival in the American College Industry,* forthcoming, 1973.

tended by students of different social classes, and even within the same school, do not arise by accident. Rather, they stem from the fact that the educational objectives and expectations of administrators, teachers, and parents, and the responsiveness of students to various patterns of teaching and control, differ for students of different social classes.* Further, class inequalities in school socialization patterns are reinforced by inequalities in financial resources. The paucity of financial support for the education of children from working-class families leaves more resources to be devoted to the children of those with commanding roles in the economy; it also forces upon the teachers and school administrators in the working-class schools a type of social relations that fairly closely mirrors that of the factory. Thus financial considerations in poorly supported working-class schools militate against small intimate classes, against a multiplicity of elective courses and specialized teachers (except disciplinary personnel), and preclude the amounts of free time for the teachers and free space required for a more open, flexible educational environment. The lack of financial support all but requires that students be treated as raw materials on a production line; it places a high premium on obedience and punctuality; there are few opportunities for independent, creative work or individualized attention by teachers. The well-financed schools attended by the children of the rich can offer much greater opportunities for the development of the capacity for sustained independent work and the other characteristics required for adequate job performance in the upper levels of the occupational hierarchy.

The correspondence between the social relations of production and the social relations of childhood sociali-

*That working-class parents seem to favor more authoritarian educational methods is perhaps a reflection of their own work experiences that have demonstrated that submission to authority is an essential ingredient in one's ability to get and hold a steady, well-paying job.

zation itself is not, however, confined to schooling. There is strong evidence for a similar correspondence in the structure of family life. The male-dominated family, with its structure of power and privilege, further articulated according to age, replicates many of the aspects of the hierarchy of production in the firm. Yet more relevant for our immediate concerns here is the evidence on social class, parental values, and childrearing practices. Most clearly directed to our formulation is Melvin Kohn's massive ten-year study, under the sponsorship of the National Institute for Mental Health.[85] Kohn's major results are that "middle class parents . . . are more likely to emphasize children's self-direction, and working class parents to emphasize their *conformity to external authority*. . . . The essential difference between the terms, as we use them, is that self-direction focuses on *internal* standards of direction for behavior; conformity focuses on *externally* imposed rules." Thus parents of lower status children value obedience, neatness, and honesty in their children, while higher status parents emphasize curiosity, self-control, and happiness. Kohn concludes: "In this exceptionally diverse society—deeply marked by racial and religious division, highly varied in economy, geography, and even degree of urbanization—social class stands out as more important for men's values than does any other line of demarcation, unaffected by all the rest of them, and apparently more important than all of them together."[86]

To refine the relation between social class, values, and childrearing, Kohn classifies his test subjects (fourteen hundred in number) according to the amount of "occupational self-direction" inherent in their jobs—using as indices whether the worker is closely supervised, whether the worker deals with things, data, or people, and whether the job is complex or repetitive. His analysis

85. Melvin L. Kohn, *Class and Conformity: A Study in Values* (Homewood, Ill.: Dorsey, 1969).

86. Ibid., p. 72.

indicates that the "relationship of social class to parents' valuation of self-direction or conformity for children is largely attributable to class-correlated variation in men's exercise of self-direction in work."[87]And he concludes:

Whether consciously or not, parents tend to impart to their children lessons derived from the conditions of life of their own social class—and thus help prepare their children for a similar class position. . . . Class differences in parental values and child rearing practices influence the development of the capacities that children will some-day need. . . . The family, then, functions as a mechanism for perpetuating inequality.

Such differential patterns of childrearing do affect more than the worker's personality and aspiration level. They also determine his or her style of self-presentation: patterns of class loyalties and modes of speech, dress, and interpersonal behavior. While such traits are by no means fixed into adulthood, their stability over the life cycle appears sufficient to account for the observed degree of intergenerational status transmission.

6. THE FAILURE OF LIBERAL SOCIAL REFORM AND THE FUTURE OF THE STRATIFICATION SYSTEM

Social Reform in the 1960s:
An Action Critique of Liberal Theory

In 1847 Karl Marx and Friedrich Engels wrote, "Wherever the bourgeoisie has risen to power, it has destroyed all feudal, patriarchal, and idyllic relationships . . . it has left no other bond betwixt man and man but crude self-interest and unfeeling 'cash payment' "[88] Ironically the positive aspect of this historic pronouncement lies at the

87.Ibid. p. 163.
88.Karl Marx and Friedrich Engels, *Communist Manifesto* (New York: International Publishers, 1948).

base of the liberal theory of stratification. Thus John Gardner, president of the Carnegie Corporation, later to become Secretary of the U.S. Department of Health, Education, and Welfare, could confidently state: "Most human societies have been beautifully organized to keep good men down. . . . Birth determined occupation and status. . . . Such societies were doomed by the Industrial Revolution."[89]

But by the early 1960s it was painfully evident that the heralded natural trend toward equality had not fared well. Despite phenomenal economic growth, a vast expansion (and equalization) of the educational system, and the introduction of the "progressive" income tax, Social Security, and other welfare state programs inequality of income has remained essentially unchanged.[90] The introduction of taxes on inheritance has done little to alter the distribution of wealth: the top one-half of one percent of wealth holders hold about a quarter of all wealth; the top one percent hold about three-quarters of all corporate stock.[91] Woman's suffrage and a more liberal attitude toward "the woman's place" in the home and on the job did not prevent a decline in the economic situation of women relative to men.[92] The attenuation of racial prejudice—attested to in numerous recent surveys—and the dramatic educational gains made by blacks have not resulted in occupational or income gains for blacks relative

89. John W. Gardner, *Excellence* (New York: Harper and Bros., 1961).

90. Gabriel Kolko, *Wealth and Power in America* (New York: Frederick A. Praeger, 1962); Herman Miller, "Income Distribution in the United States, 1960 Census," mimeographed (Washington, D.C.: U.S. Government Printing Office, 1966).

91. Robert Lampman, *The Share of Top Wealth Holders in the National Wealth* (Princeton, N.J.: Princeton University Press, 1962).

92. Richard C. Edwards, Michael Reich, and Thomas Weisskopf, *The Capitalist System* (Englewood Cliffs, N.J.: Prentice-Hall, 1972), p. 324.

to whites.[93] Finally the extension of public elementary
and secondary education and the growth of state supported higher education have not been accompanied by
a reduction in the extent to which one's family's social
status determines one's own education opportunities.[94]
Similarly the correlation between the occupational status
of individuals and their parents has not been reduced.[95]

Viewing this panorama of persistent inequality, the liberal community of the 1960s grew to emphasize ever
more heavily the age-old distinction between inequality
of *opportunity* and inequality of *outcome.* According to this
perspective, inequality of outcome (income, wealth,
status, and job desirability) is necessitated by the very
structure of industrial society[96] whose harshest effects
can be no more than ameliorated through enlightened
social welfare practices. The vital progressive thrust of
liberal social policy, according to the same perspective,
must grow from the sobering necessity of limiting our
aspirations as to equality of outcome, while setting our
highest sights on providing all with a fair shot at unequal
economic reward. According to this view, the justness of
the social order can then be assessed by the extent to
which it has eliminated discrimination based on social
background, caste, or color.

In this liberal perspective the capitalist economy,
finally shorn of anachronistic prejudices, can become the
true meritocracy. The "performance orientation" and
"organizational rationality" of employers, the imperson-
ality of labor markets, and the "structural differentiation

93. Michael Reich, "The Economics of Racism," in *Problems in
Political Economy,* ed. David M. Gordon, (Lexington, Mass.: D.C.
Heath, 1971).

94. William G. Spady, "Educational Mobility and Access:
Growth and Paradoxes," *American Journal of Sociology,* November
1967; Blau and Duncan, *The American Occupational Structure.*

95. Blau and Duncan, *The American Occupational Structure.*

96. Parsons, "Evolutionary Universals in Society"; Davis and
Moore, "Some Principles of Stratification."

of the economic sub-system" all conspire to eliminate sexual, racial, and social class discriminations. Intergenerational status transmission, in this view, thus comes to depend integrally on inherited (whether through nature or nurture) differences in ability and willingness to perform. Thus Gardner can confidently assert, in the same breath, that "when a society gives up hereditary stratification . . . dramatic differences in ability and performance . . . emerge . . . and may lead to peaks and valleys of status as dramatic as those produced by hereditary stratification."[97]

Thus the decade of the 1960s was marked by the commitment to bring social policy to bear on the equalization of opportunity. In fulfilling this commitment, liberal social policy has drawn on liberal social theory in three essential respects. First, it has harbored an abiding optimism, flowing from the theorists' separation of equality of opportunity and equality of outcome. The hierarchical division of labor could be maintained while the atavistic remains of bigotry and unequal social resources could be swept away via additional legislation and more effective propaganda. Second, the technocratic orientation of liberal theory indicated that the crucial policy variables were those related to differences in cognitive and psychomotor performance related skills—hence the emphasis on education and training. This, then, provided the focus of the reforms of the 1960s. Third, the limits of social reform in this area, so the theory predicts, are dictated by genetic differences in ability.

A less auspicious set of assumptions could scarcely have been chosen, for the cognitive abilities central to the theory have turned out to be far less socially malleable than the liberals had hoped. By 1970 the hubris of the War on Poverty, in the face of persistent failure, had vanished. In the area of educational policy, the "empirical finding" that differing levels of resources did not sig-

97. Gardner, *Excellence.*

nificantly promote scholastic achievement[98] was quickly
buttressed by a host of dismal assessments of the performance of the major compensatory educational programs
—Title 1, Head Start, Follow Through, and others.[99]

These failures, of course, softened the liberal position
for the inevitable conservative counterattack. This
counterattack has been based on both pillars of the liberal theory of stratification: *willingness* and *ability* to perform in the impersonal industrial marketplace. The vogu-
ish "culture of poverty" school locates the blame for
poverty in deeply rooted deficiencies of the poor themselves, limiting their willingness to perform.[100] Progressive social theory has been unable to defend itself against
this thrust, as it lacks a firm understanding of the structural relations between the cultural subsystems in the
workplace and in the larger society.[101] The assault of the
"genetic school" discussed in this paper is based on the
purported *inability* of the poor to perform. The proponents of liberal social policy cannot defend itself against

98. Coleman et al., *Equality of Educational Opportunity;* Frederick
Mostellar and Daniel P. Moynihan, *On Equality of Educational
Opportunity* (New York: Random House, 1972). Whether additional school resources are in fact irrelevant to greater academic
performance is still an unsettled question. See Samuel Bowles
and Henry Levin, "The Determinants of Scholastic Achievement: An Appraisal of Some Recent Evidence," *Journal of Human
Resources* 3 (Winter 1968); James Guthrie et al., *Schools and Inequality* (Cambridge, Mass.: MIT Press, 1971). Available studies
shed no light whatsoever on the relation between school resources and performance outside the cognitive sphere.

99. Harvey Averch et al., *How Effective Is Schooling? A Critical
Review and Synthesis of Research Findings* (Santa Monica: The
RAND Corporation, 1972); David Armor, "The Evidence on
Busing," *The Public Interest* (Summer 1972); T. Ribich, *Poverty and
Education* (Washington, D.C.: The Brookings Institute, 1968).

100. Edward Banfield, *The Unheavenly City* (Boston: Little,
Brown, 1968); Oscar Lewis, "The Culture of Poverty"; Daniel P.
Moynihan, *The Negro Family: The Case for National Action* (Cam-
bridge, Mass.: MIT Press, 1967).

101. Herbert Gans, *The Urban Villagers* (New York: Macmillan,
1962); Greer, *The Great School Legend*.

the massive attack of the geneticists without reversing in midstream; for it had consistently posited "ability" and "performance" as the ideal criteria of employability and economic reward. This perspective has manifested itself particularly strongly in the more policy-related social science disciplines, especially in the economics and sociology of education. Thus the economic returns to schooling have been "corrected for ability differences,"[102] student quality has been measured by I Q, and school quality by contribution to cognitive achievement,[103] and cognitive indices have been taken as the basic output variables in educational production functions.[104] In the area of social policy the findings of the Coleman report,[105] relying only on measures of cognitive achievement, were conceived, and are still consistently referred to, as basic to the solution to problems of poverty and inequality. Thus Moynihan and Mosteller, in the introduction to their massive reanalysis of the Coleman data, refer to the report as a "revolutionary document" whose crowning achievement lies in its taking "educational output, not input alone . . . (as) the central issue."[106] Adding the

102. Zvi Griliches, "Notes on the Role of Education in Production Functions and Growth Accounting," in *Education, Income and Human Capital*, Studies in Income and Wealth, ed. W. Lee Hansen, vol. 35 (New York: National Bureau of Economic Research, 1970); Weiss, "The Effect of Education on the Earnings of Blacks and Whites."

103. For example, Alexander W. Astin, "Undergraduate Achievement and Institutional 'Excellence,' " *Science* 161 (August 1968). For a survey see Bowles, "Unequal Education and the Reproduction of the Social Division of Labor."

104. Thus Averch et al., in *How Effective Is Schooling?*, their RAND Corporation report to the President's Commission on School Finance, report: "[In our attempt] to assess the current state of knowledge regarding the determinants of educational effectiveness . . . [we find that] educational outcomes are almost exclusively measured by cognitive achievement" (p. ix).

105. Coleman et al., *Equality of Educational Opportunity*.

106. Mosteller and Moynihan, *On Equality of Educational Opportunity*, p. 27.

critics of Jensen and Herrnstein to this list, we are faced with a degree of unanimity perhaps unparalleled in social science.

In earlier sections we argued that the liberal perspective on stratification is incorrect. Hence we are not surprised that social policy based on its premises have failed. Nor are we surprised at the success of the counterattack. The theoretical fallacy at the heart of liberal stratification theory, stated in policy-oriented terms, is the assertion that equality of opportunity is compatible with equality of outcomes. We have argued that neither "ability" nor "willingness" can be understood outside a total perspective in which social, racial, ethnic, and sexual differentiations and differential patterns of socialization interact with the hierarchical division of labor. Individuals, as well as their social subcultures, develop according to their relationship to the social division of labor. Our argument holds that the social relations of production are mirrored —via the correspondence principles—in the basic socialization agencies of family, community, and school. Thus inequality of opportunity is a by-product of the organization of production itself, and cannot be attached either to "dysfunctional" attributes of the underclasses or the self-interested malfeasance and unfeeling perversity of unprogressive social policy. In addition to performance-related individual capacities normally developed on a class basis, beneath the surface of rationality, meritocracy, and performance-oriented efficiency, the capitalist economic system operates on a subtle network of ascriptions and symbolic differentiations, quite as well-articulated as the most complex caste system. Moreover, this "open caste system" is essential to the legitimation and operation of the hierarchical division of labor itself. Any particular element may be eliminated (e.g., racism), but new modes of status differentiation must arise to take its place. Such is the logic of our argument.

Contradictory Development and the Future of the Class Structure

We have described the stratification system in the United States as a reflection of the hierarchical division of labor. Moreover, we have exhibited a strong tendency for the social system to draw on abiding status and caste distinctions (including race, sex, ethnicity, and personal demeanor) in the legitimation of the capitalist social relations of production, while creating other distinctions (e.g., I Q educational credentials) when necessary toward these same ends. Yet our analysis must be incomplete in one essential respect: it seems to propose that the system has little difficulty in fulfilling these preconditions for its own reproduction. Yet the political and social upheavals of the 1960s—including the black and women's movements, radical student revolts, rank-and-file unrest in the labor movement, the rise of the counterculture, and a new mood of equality among youth—have ushered in a growing consciousness directed against the stratification system, and even the hierarchical division of labor itself.[107] Clearly our analysis has been one-sided.

The problem? We have treated only the way in which the United States capitalist system reproduces itself, without dealing with the contradictions that inevitably arise out of the system's own successes—contradictions that lead to social dislocation and require structural change in the social relations of production for the fur-

107. Dan Gilbarg and David Finkelhor, *Up against the American Myth* (New York: Holt, Rinehart and Winston, 1970); Edwards, Reich, and Weisskopf, *The Capitalist System;* Gintis, "New Working Class and Revolutionary Youth"; Bowles, "Contradictions in U.S. Higher Education"; Theodore Roszak, *The Making of the Counter-Culture* (New York: Doubleday, 1969).

ther development of the social system.[108] The present seems to represent one of these crucial periods of contradiction.[109] We can do no more here than list some of these central contradictions.

First, the legitimacy of the capitalist system has been historically based in no small part on its ability to "deliver the goods." The ever increasing mass of consumer goods and services seemed to promise constant improvement in levels of well-being for all. Yet the very success of the process has undermined the urgency of consumer wants; other needs—for community, for security, for a more integral and self-initiated work and social life—are coming to the fore. And these needs are unified by a common characteristic: they cannot be met simply by producing more consumer goods and services. On the contrary, the economic foundations of capital accumulation are set firmly in the destruction of the social basis for the satisfaction of these needs. Thus through "economic development" itself, needs are generated that the advanced capitalist system is not geared to satisfy.[110] Thus the legitimacy of the capitalist order must increasingly be handled by other social mechanisms, of which the meritocracy is a major element. It is not clear that the latter can bear this strain.

Second, the concentration of capital and the continuing separation of workers—white collar and professional as well as manual—from control over the production process has reduced the natural defenders of the capitalist

108. On "reproduction" and "contradiction" in the analysis of the social system, see Herbert Gintis, "Counter-Culture and Political Activism," *Telos* (Summer 1972).

109. For a more extended treatment of the contradictions of advanced United States capitalism, see Bowles, "Contradictions in U.S. Higher Education"; Gintis, "Counter-Culture and Political Activism."

110. For a more complete statement of their position, see Gintis, "Education and the Characteristics of Worker Productivity"; Bowles, "Contradictions in U.S. Higher Education."

order to a small minority.[111] Two hundred years ago over three-fourths of white families owned land, tools, or other productive property; this fraction has fallen to about a third, and even among this group, a tiny minority owns the lion's share of all productive property. Similarly two hundred years ago about all white male workers were their own boss. The demise of the family farm, the artisan shop, and the small store, and the rise of the modern corporation, has reduced the figure to less than 10 percent.[112] For most Americans the capitalist system has come to mean someone *else's* right to profits, someone *else's* right to work unbossed and in pursuit of one's own objectives. The decline of groups outside the wage labor system—farmer, artisan, entrepreneur, and independent professional—has eliminated a ballast of capitalist support, leaving the legitimation system alone to divide strata among the working class against one another.

Third, developments in technology and work organization have begun to undermine the main line of ideological defense of the capitalist system, namely, the idea that the capitalist relations of production—private property and the hierarchical organization of work—are the most conducive to the rapid expansion of productivity.[113] Repeated experiments have shown that in those complex work tasks that increasingly dominate modern production, participatory control by workers is a more productive form of work organization.[114] The boredom and stultification of the production line and the steno pool, the

111. For a more elaborate statement of this problem, see Schumpeter, *Imperialism and Social Class;* Bowles, "Contradictions in U.S. Higher Education."

112. See Jackson T. Main, *The Social Structure of Revolutionary America* (Princeton, N.J.: Princeton University Press, 1965); Reich in *The Capitalist System,* eds. Edwards, Reich, and Weisskopf.

113. See Gorz, "Capitalist Relations of Production and the Socially Necessary Labor Force."

114. The evidence is summarized in Gintis, "Power and Alienation."

shackled creativity of technical workers and teachers, the
personal frustration of the bureaucratic office routine,
increasingly lose their claim as the price of material com-
fort. The ensuing attacks on bureaucratic oppression go
hand in hand with demystification of the meritocracy
ideology as discussed in this paper. Support for capitalist
institutions—once firmly rooted in their claim to superiority in meeting urgent consumption needs and squarely
based on a broad mass of property-owning independent
workers—is thus weakened by the process of capitalist
development itself. At the same time powerful anticapitalist forces are brought into being. The accumulation of
capital—the engine of growth under capitalism—has as
its necessary companion the proletarianization of labor.
The continuing integration of new groups into the worldwide wage labor system has not brought about the international working-class consciousness that many Marxists
had predicted. But the process has introduced serious
strains into the capitalist order. These may be summarized as a fourth and fifth set of contradictions.

Fourth, the international expansion of capital has
fueled nationalists and anticapitalist movements in many
of the poor countries. The strains associated with the
worldwide integration of the capitalist system are manifested in the resistance of the people of Vietnam, in the
rise of the Chilean left, in the socialist revolution in China
and Cuba, and in political instability and guerrilla movements elsewhere in Asia, Africa, and Latin America. The
United States role in opposition to wars of national liber-
ation—particularly in Vietnam—has brought part of the
struggle back home and exacerbated many of the domestic contradictions of advanced capitalism.[115]

Fifth, and cutting across all of the above, with the return to comparatively smooth capitalist development in

115. See Therborn, reprinted in *The Capitalist System*, eds. Edwards, Relch, and Weisskopf.

the United States in the mid-1950s after the tumultuous decades of the 1930s and 1940s, the impact of far-reaching cumulative changes in the class structure is increasingly reflected in crises of public consciousness. The corporatization of agriculture and reduction of the farm population has particularly affected blacks, who are subjected to the painful process of forceful integration into the urban wage labor system. The resulting political instabilities are not unlike those following the vast wave of immigrants in the early decades of the century. Changes in the technology of household production and the vast increase in female labor in the service industries also portend a radically altered economic position of women. Finally the large corporation and the state bureaucracies have replaced entrepreneurial, elite white-collar, and independent professional jobs as the locus of middle-class economic activity, and the effective proletarianization of white-collar labor marks the already advanced integration of these groups into the wage labor system.[116] In each case contradictions have arisen between the traditional consciousness of these groups and their new objective economic situations. This has provided much of the impetus for radical movements among blacks, women, students, and counter culture youth.

While searching for long-range structural accommodations to these contradictions, defenders of the capitalist order will likely be forced to place increasing reliance on the general legitimation mechanisms associated with the meritocratic-technocratic ideology. As a result it appears likely that the future will reveal increasing reliance on the "meritocratic" stratification mechanisms and the associated legitimating ideologies: IQ-ism and educational credentialism. Efforts and resources will doubtless multi-

---

116. See Bowles, "Contradictions in U.S. Higher Education"; Gintis, "New Working Class and Revolutionary Youth"; Gintis, "Counter-Culture and Political Activism."

ply toward the "full equalization of opportunity," but the results, if our arguments are correct, will be limited as long as the hierarchical division of labor perpetuates itself.

The credentialist and IQ ideology upon which the "meritocratic" legitimation mechanisms depend is thus already under attack. Blacks reject the racism implicit in much of the recent work on IQ; they are not mystified by the elaborate empirical substantiation of the geneticist position, nor by the assertions of meritocracy by functionalist sociologists. Their daily experience gives them insights that seem to have escaped many social scientists. Likewise women—indeed many poor people of both sexes—know that their exclusion from jobs is not based on any deficiency of educational credentials.

We have here attempted to speed up the process of demystification by showing that the purportedly "scientific" empirical basis of credentialism and IQ-ism is false. In addition, we have attempted to facilitate linkages between these groups and workers' movements within the dominant white male labor force, by showing that the *same* mechanisms are used to divide strata against one another so as to maintain the inferior status of "minority" groups.

The assault on economic inequality and hierarchical control of work appears likely to intensify. Along with other social strains endemic to advanced capitalism, the growing tension between people's needs for self-realization in work and the needs of capitalists and managers for secure top-down control of economic activity opens up the possibility of powerful social movements dedicated to the elimination of the hierarchical division of labor. We hope our paper will contribute to this outcome.

The Fallacy of
Richard Herrnstein's IQ

NOAM CHOMSKY

Harvard psychologist Richard Herrnstein's by now well-
known *Atlantic* article, "IQ" (September 1971), has been
the subject of considerable controversy. Unfortunately
this has tended to extend the currency of his ideas rather
than to mitigate against them! Herrnstein purports to
show that American society is drifting toward a stable
hereditary meritocracy, with social stratification by inborn differences and a corresponding distribution of "rewards." The argument is based on the hypothesis that
differences in mental abilities are inherited and that people close in mental ability are more likely to marry and
reproduce,* so that there will be a tendency toward long-
term stratification by mental ability, which Herrnstein
takes to be measured by IQ. Second, Herrnstein argues
that "success" requires mental ability and that social rewards "depend on success." This step in the argument
embodies two assumptions: first, it is so in fact; and,
second, it must be so for society to function effectively.
The conclusion is that there is a tendency toward hereditary meritocracy, with "social standing" (which reflects
earnings and prestige) concentrated in groups with

SOURCE: Noam Chomsky, "The Fallacy of Richard Herrnstein's IQ," *Social Policy* 3, no. 1 (May-June 1972).

*He does not specifically mention this assumption, but it is
necessary to the argument.

higher IQs. The tendency will be accelerated as society becomes more egalitarian, that is, as artificial social barriers are eliminated, defects in prenatal (e.g., nutritional) environment are overcome, and so on, so that natural ability can play a more direct role in attainment of social reward. Therefore, as society becomes more egalitarian, social rewards will be concentrated in a hereditary meritocratic elite.

Herrnstein has been widely denounced as a racist for this argument, a conclusion that seems to me unwarranted. There is, however, an ideological element in his argument that is absolutely critical to it. Consider the second step, that is, the claim that IQ is a factor in attaining reward and that this must be so for society to function effectively. Herrnstein recognizes that his argument will collapse if, indeed, society can be organized in accordance with the "socialist dictum, 'From each according to his ability, to each according to his needs.' " His argument would not apply in a society in which "income (economic, social, and political) is unaffected by success."

Actually Herrnstein fails to point out that his argument requires the assumption not only that success must be rewarded, but that it must be rewarded in quite specific ways. If individuals are rewarded for success only by prestige, then no conclusions of any importance follow. It will only follow (granting his other assumptions) that children of people who are respected for their own achievements will be more likely to be respected for their own achievements, an innocuous result even if true. It may be that the child of two Olympic swimmers has a greater than average chance of achieving the same success (and the acclaim for it), but no dire social consequences follow from this hypothesis. The conclusion that Herrnstein and others find disturbing is that wealth and power will tend to concentrate in a hereditary meritocracy. But this follows only on the assumption that wealth and power (not merely respect) must be the rewards of successful achievement and that these (or their effects) are transmitted from parents to children. The issue is confused by Herrnstein's failure to isolate the specific factors crucial to his argument and his use of the phrase "income" (economic, social, and political) to cover "rewards" of all types, including respect as well as wealth. It is confused further by the fact that he continually slips into identifying "social standing" with wealth. Thus he writes that if the social ladder is tapered steeply, the obvious way to rescue the people at the bottom is "to increase the aggregate wealth of society so that there is more room at the top"—which is untrue if "social standing" is a matter of acclaim and respect. (We overlook the fact that even on his tacit assumption redistribution of income would appear to be an equally obvious strategy.)

Consider then the narrower assumption that is crucial to his argument: transmittable wealth and power accrue to mental ability and must do so for society to function effectively. If this assumption is false and society can be organized more or less in accordance with the socialist dictum, then nothing is left of Herrnstein's argument (except that it will apply to a competitive society in which his other factual assumptions hold). But the assumption is true, Herrnstein claims. The reason is that ability "expresses itself in labor only for gain" and people "compete for gain—economic and otherwise." People will work only if they are rewarded in terms of "social and political influence or relief from threat." All of this is merely asserted; no justification is given for these assertions. Note again that the argument supports the disturbing conclusions he draws only if we identify the "gain" for which people allegedly compete as transmittable wealth and power.

What reason is there to believe the crucial assumption that people will work only for gain in (transmittable) wealth and power, so that society cannot be organized in accordance with the socialist dictum? In a decent society everyone would have the opportunity to find interesting work, and each person would be permitted the fullest

possible scope for his talents. Would more be required—
in particular, extrinsic reward in the form of wealth and
power? Only if we assume that applying one's talents in
interesting and socially useful work is not rewarding in
itself, that there is no intrinsic satisfaction in creative and
productive work, suited to one's abilities, or in helping
others (say, one's family, friends, associates, or simply
fellow members of society). Unless we suppose this, then
even granting all of Herrnstein's other assumptions, it
does not follow that there should be any concentration of
wealth or power or influence in a hereditary elite.

For Herrnstein's argument to have any force at all we
must assume that people labor only for gain, and that the
satisfaction in interesting or socially beneficial work or in
work well done or in the respect shown to such activities
is not a sufficient "gain" to induce anyone to work. The
assumption, in short, is that without material reward people will vegetate. For this crucial assumption no sem-
blance of an argument is offered. Rather Herrnstein
merely asserts that if bakers and lumberjacks "got the top
salaries and the top social approval"* in place of those
now at the top of the social ladder, then "the scale of IQs
would also invert," and the most talented would strive to
become bakers and lumberjacks. This, of course, is no
argument, but merely a reiteration of the claim that
necessarily individuals work only for extrinsic reward.
Furthermore, it is an extremely implausible claim. I
doubt very much that Herrnstein would become a baker
or lumberjack if he could earn more money in that way.

Similar points have been made in commentary on
Herrnstein's article,[1] but in response he merely reiterates

---

*Note again Herrnstein's failure to distinguish remuneration
from social approval, though the argument collapses if the only
reward is approval.

1. *Atlantic*, November 1971. See p. 110, first paragraph, for his
rejoinder.

his belief that there is no way "to end the blight of differential rewards." Continued assertion, however, is not to be confused with argument. Herrnstein's further assertion that "history shows . . ." in effect concedes defeat. Of course, history shows concentration of wealth and power in the hands of those able to accumulate it. One thought Herrnstein was trying to do more than merely put forth this truism. By reducing his argument finally to this assertion, Herrnstein implicitly concedes that he has no justification for the crucial assumption on which his argument rests, the unargued and unsupported claim that the talented must receive higher rewards.

If we look more carefully at what history and experience show, we find that if free exercise is permitted to the combination of ruthlessness, cunning, and whatever other qualities provide "success" in competitive societies, then those who have these qualities will rise to the top and will use their wealth and power to preserve and extend the privileges they attain. They will also construct ideologies to demonstrate that this result is only fair and just. We also find, contrary to capitalist ideology and behaviorist doctrine (of the nontautological variety), that many people often do not act solely or even primarily so as to achieve material gain or to maximize applause. As for the argument (if offered) that "history shows" the untenability of the "socialist dictum" that Herrnstein must reject for his argument to be valid, this may be assigned the same status as an eighteenth-century argument to the effect that capitalist democracy is impossible, as history shows.

One sometimes reads arguments to the effect that people are "economic maximizers," as we can see from the fact that given the opportunity, some will accumulate material reward and power.[2] By similar logic we could

2. See, e.g., Harry W. Blair, "The Green Revolution and 'Economic Man': Some Lessons for Community Development in

prove that people are psychopathic criminals, since given social conditions under which those with violent criminal tendencies were free from all restraints, they might very well accumulate power and wealth while nonpsychopaths suffer in servitude. Evidently from the lessons of history we can reach only the most tentative conclusions about basic human tendencies.

Suppose that Herrnstein's unargued and crucial claim is incorrect. Suppose that there is, in fact, some intrinsic satisfaction in employing one's talents in challenging and creative work. Then, one might argue, this should compensate even for a diminution of extrinsic reward; and "reinforcement" should be given for the performance of unpleasant and boring tasks. It follows then that there should be a concentration of wealth (and the power that comes from wealth) among the less talented. I do not urge this conclusion, but merely observe that it is more plausible than Herrnstein's if his fundamental and unsupported assumption is false.

The belief that people must be driven or drawn to work by "gain" is a curious one. Of course, it is true if we use the vacuous Skinnerian scheme and speak of the "reinforcing quality" of interesting or useful work; and it may be true, though irrelevant to Herrnstein's thesis, if the "gain" sought is merely general respect and prestige. The assumption necessary for Herrnstein's argument, namely, that people must be driven or drawn to work by reward of wealth or power, obviously does not derive from science, nor does it appear to be supported by personal experience. I suspect that Herrnstein would exclude himself from the generalization, as already noted. Thus I am not convinced that he would at once apply for a job as a garbage collector if this were to pay more than his present position as a teacher and research psychologist. He would say, I am sure, that he does his work not because it maximizes wealth (or even prestige) but because it is interesting and challenging, that is, intrinsically rewarding; and there is no reason to doubt that this response would be correct. The statistical evidence, he points out, suggests that "if very high income is your goal, and you have a high IQ, do not waste your time with formal education beyond high school." Thus if you are an economic maximizer, don't bother with a college education, given a high IQ. Few follow this advice, quite probably because they prefer interesting work to mere material reward. The assumption that people will work only for gain in wealth and power is not only unargued but quite probably false, except under extreme deprivation. But this degrading and brutal assumption, common to capitalist ideology and the behaviorist view of human beings, is fundamental to Herrnstein's argument.

There are other ideological elements in Herrnstein's argument, more peripheral, but still worth noting. He invariably describes the society he sees evolving as a "meritocracy," thus expressing the value judgment that the characteristics that yield reward are a sign of merit, that is, positive characteristics. He considers specifically IQ, but, of course, recognizes that there might very well be other factors in the attainment of "social success." One might speculate, rather plausibly, that wealth and power tend to accrue to those who are ruthless, cunning, avaricious, self-seeking, lacking in sympathy and compassion, subservient to authority, willing to abandon principle for material gain, and so on. Furthermore, these traits might very well be as heritable as IQ and might outweigh IQ as factors in gaining material reward. Such qualities might be just the valuable ones for a war of all against all. If so, then the society that results (applying Herrnstein's "syllogism") could hardly be characterized as a "meritocracy." By using the word "meritocracy" Herrnstein begs some interesting questions and reveals implicit assumptions about our society that are hardly self-evident.

Teachers in ghetto schools commonly observe that students who are self-reliant, imaginative, energetic, and unwilling to submit to authority are often regarded as troublemakers and punished, on occasion even driven out of the school system. The implicit assumption that in a highly discriminatory society, or one with tremendous inequality of wealth and power, the "meritorious" will be rewarded is a curious one, indeed.

Consider further Herrnstein's assumption that, in fact, social rewards accrue to those who perform beneficial and needed services. He claims that the "gradient of occupations" is "a natural measure of value and scarcity," and that "the ties among IQ, occupation, and social standing make practical sense." This is his way of expressing the familiar theory that people are automatically rewarded in a just society (and more or less in our society) in accordance with their contribution to social welfare or "output." The theory is familiar, and so are its fallacies. Given great inequalities of wealth, we will expect to find that the "gradient of occupations" by pay is a natural measure of service to wealth and power—to those who can purchase and compel—and only by accident "a natural measure of value." The ties among IQ, occupation, and social standing that Herrnstein notes make "practical sense" for those with wealth and power, but not necessarily for society or its members in general.*

The point is quite obvious. Herrnstein's failure to notice it is particularly surprising given the data on which he bases his observations about the relation between social reward and occupation. He bases these judgments on

---

*To assume that society tends to reward those who perform a social service is to succumb to essentially the same fallacy (among others) that undermines the argument that a free market, in principle, leads to optimal satisfaction of wants—whereas when wealth is badly distributed, the system will tend to produce luxuries for the few who can pay rather than necessities for the many who cannot.

a ranking of occupations that shows, for example, that
accountants, specialists in public relations, auditors, and
sales managers tend to have higher IQs (hence, he would
claim, receive higher pay, as they must if society is to
function effectively) than musicians, riveters, bakers,
lumberjacks, and teamsters. Accountants were ranked
highest among seventy-four listed occupations, with public relations fourth, musicians thirty-fifth, riveters fiftieth,
bakers sixty-fifth, truck drivers sixty-seventh, and lumberjacks seventieth. From such data Herrnstein concludes that society is wisely "husbanding its intellectual
resources"* and that the gradient of occupation is a natural measure of value and makes practical sense. Is it obvious that an accountant helping a corporation to cut its tax
bill is doing work of greater social value than a musician,
riveter, baker, truck driver, or lumberjack? Is a lawyer
who earns a $100,000 fee to keep a dangerous drug on
the market worth more to society than a farm worker or
a nurse? Is a surgeon who performs operations for the
rich doing work of greater social value than a practitioner
in the slums who may work much harder for much less
extrinsic reward? The gradient of occupations that
Herrnstein uses to support his claims with regard to the
correlation between IQ and social value surely reflects, in
part at least, the demands of wealth and power; a further
argument is needed to demonstrate Herrnstein's claim
that those at the top of the list are performing the highest

---

*Misleadingly Herrnstein states: "Society is, in effect, hus-
banding its intellectual resources by holding engineers in
greater esteem and paying them more." But if he really wants to
claim this on the basis of the ties between IQ and social standing
that his data reveal, then he should conclude as well that society
is husbanding its intellectual resources by holding accountants
and PR men in greater esteem and paying them more. Quite
apart from this, it is not so obvious as he apparently believes that
society is wisely husbanding its intellectual resources by employing most of its scientists and engineers in military and space
research and development.

service to "society," which is wisely husbanding its resources by rewarding the accountants and public relations experts and engineers (e.g., designers of antipersonnel weapons) for their special skills. Herrnstein's failure to notice what his data immediately suggest is another indication of his uncritical (and apparently unconscious) acceptance of capitalist ideology in its crudest form.

Notice that if the ranking of occupations by IQ correlates with ranking by income, then the data that Herrnstein cite can be interpreted in part as an indication of an unfortunate bias toward occupations that serve the wealthy and powerful and away from work that might be more satisfying and socially useful. At least this would certainly seem a plausible assumption, one that Herrnstein never discusses, given his unquestioning acceptance of the prevailing ideology.

There is, no doubt, some complex of characteristics conducive to material reward in a state capitalist society. This complex may include IQ and quite possibly other more important factors, perhaps those noted earlier. To the extent that these characteristics are heritable (and a factor in choosing mates) there will be a tendency toward stratification in terms of these qualities. This much is obvious enough.

Furthermore, people with higher IQs will tend to have more freedom in selection of occupation. Depending on their other traits and opportunities, they will tend to choose more interesting work or more remunerative work, these categories being by no means identical. Therefore, one can expect to find some correlation between IQ and material reward, and some correlation between IQ and an independent ranking of occupations by their intrinsic interest and intellectual challenge. Were we to rank occupations by social utility in some manner, we would probably find at most a weak correlation with remuneration or with intrinsic interest and quite possibly a negative correlation. Unequal distribution of wealth and power will naturally introduce a bias toward greater remuneration for services to the privileged, thereby causing the scale of remuneration to diverge from the scale of social utility in many instances.

From Herrnstein's data and arguments we can draw no further conclusions about what would happen in a just society, unless we add the assumption that people labor only for material gain, for wealth and power, and that they do not seek interesting work suited to their abilities —that they would vegetate rather than do such work. Since Herrnstein offers no reason why we should believe any of this (and there is certainly some reason why we should not), none of his conclusions follow from his factual assumptions, even if these are correct. The crucial step in his syllogism in effect amounts to the claim that the ideology of capitalist society expresses universal traits of human nature, and that certain related assumptions of behaviorist psychology are correct. Conceivably these unsupported assumptions are true. But once it is recognized how critical their role is in his argument and what empirical support they, in fact, have, any further interest in this argument would seem to evaporate.

I have assumed so far that prestige, respect, and so on might be factors in causing people to work (as Herrnstein implies). This seems to me by no means obvious, though even if it is true, Herrnstein's conclusions clearly do not follow. In a decent society socially necessary and unpleasant work would be divided on some egalitarian basis, and beyond that people would have, as an inalienable right, the widest possible opportunity to do work that interests them. They might be "reinforced" by self-respect if they do their work to the best of their ability, or if their work benefits those to whom they are related by bonds of friendship and sympathy and solidarity. Such notions are commonly an object of ridicule—as it was common, in an earlier period, to scoff at the absurd idea that a peasant has the same inalienable rights as a nobleman. There always have been, and no doubt always will be, people who cannot conceive of the possibility that things could be different from what they are. Perhaps they are right, but again one awaits a rational argument.

In a decent society of the sort just described—which, one might think, becomes increasingly realizable with technological progress—there should be no shortage of scientists, engineers, surgeons, artists, craftsmen, teachers, and so on, simply because such work is intrinsically rewarding. There is no reason to doubt that people in these occupations would work as hard as those fortunate few who can choose their own work generally do today. Of course, if Herrnstein's assumptions, borrowed from capitalist ideology and behaviorist belief, are correct, then people will remain idle rather than do such work unless there is deprivation and extrinsic reward. But no reason is suggested as to why we should accept this strange and demeaning doctrine.

Lurking in the background of the debate over Herrnstein's syllogism is the matter of race, though he himself barely alludes to it. His critics are disturbed, and rightly so, by the fact that his argument will surely be exploited by racists to justify discrimination, much as Herrnstein may personally deplore this fact. More generally Herrnstein's argument will be adopted by the privileged to justify privilege on the grounds that they are being rewarded for their ability and that such reward is necessary if society is to function properly. The situation is reminiscent of nineteenth-century racist anthropology. Marvin Harris notes:

Racism also had its uses as a justification for class and caste hierarchies; it was a splendid explanation of both national and class privilege. It helped to maintain slavery and serfdom; it smoothed the way for the rape of Africa and the slaughter of the American Indian; it steeled the nerves of the Manchester captains of industry as they lowered wages, lengthened the working day, and hired more women and children.[3]

We can expect Herrnstein's arguments to be used in a similar way and for similar reasons. When we discover that his argument is without force, unless we adopt unargued and implausible premises that happen to incorporate the dominant ideology, we quite naturally turn to the question of the social function of his conclusions and ask why the argument is taken seriously, exactly as in the case of nineteenth-century racist anthropology.

Since the issue is often obscured by polemic, it is perhaps worth stating again that the question of the validity and scientific status of a particular point of view is, of course, logically independent from the question of its social function; each is a legitimate topic of inquiry, and the latter becomes of particular interest when the point of view in question is revealed to be seriously deficient on empirical or logical grounds.

The nineteenth-century racist anthropologists were no doubt quite often honest and sincere. They might have believed that they were simply dispassionate investigators, advancing science, following the facts where they led. Conceding this, we might, nevertheless, question their judgment, and not merely because the evidence was poor and the arguments fallacious. We might take note of the relative lack of concern over the ways in which these "scientific investigations" were likely to be used. It would be a poor excuse for the nineteenth-century racist anthropologist to plead, in Herrnstein's words, that "a neutral commentator . . . would have to say that the case

3. Marvin Harris, *The Rise of Anthropological Theory* (New York: Crowell, 1968), pp. 100–101. By the 1860s, he writes, "anthropology and racial determinism had become almost synonymous."

is simply not settled" (with regard to racial inferiority) and that the "fundamental issue" is "whether inquiry shall (again) be shut off because someone thinks society is best left in ignorance." The nineteenth-century racist anthropologist, like any other person, is responsible for the effects of what he does, insofar as they can be clearly foreseen. If the likely consequences of his "scientific work" are those that Harris describes, he has the responsibility to take this likelihood into account. This would be true even if the work had real scientific merit—more so, in fact, in this case.

Similarly imagine a psychologist in Hitler's Germany who thought he could show that Jews had a genetically determined tendency toward usury (like squirrels bred to collect too many nuts) or a drive toward antisocial conspiracy and domination, and so on. If he were criticized for even undertaking these studies, could he merely respond that "a neutral commentator . . . would have to say that the case is simply not settled" and that the "fundamental issue" is "whether inquiry shall (again) be shut off because someone thinks society is best left in ignorance"? I think not. Rather I think that such a response would have been met with justifible contempt. At best he could claim that he is faced with a conflict of values. On the one hand, there is the alleged scientific importance of determining whether, in fact, Jews have a genetically determined tendency toward usury and domination (as might conceivably be the case). On the other, there is the likelihood that even opening this question and regarding it as a subject for scientific inquiry would provide ammunition for Goebbels and Rosenberg and their henchmen. Were this hypothetical psychologist to disregard the likely social consequences of his research (or even his undertaking of research) under existing social conditions, he would fully deserve the contempt of decent people. Of course, scientific curiosity should be encouraged (though fallacious argument and investigation of silly questions should not), but it is not an absolute value.

The extravagant praise lavished on Herrnstein's flimsy argument and the widespread failure to note its implicit bias and unargued assumptions[4] suggest that we are not dealing simply with a question of scientific curiosity. Since it is impossible to explain this acclaim on the basis of the substance or force of the argument, it is natural to ask whether the conclusions are so welcome to many commentators that they lose their critical faculties and fail to perceive that certain crucial and quite unsupported assumptions happen to be nothing other than a variant of the prevailing ideology. This failure is disturbing, more so, perhaps, than the conclusions Herrnstein attempts to draw from his flawed syllogism.

Turning to the question of race and intelligence, we grant too much to the contemporary investigator of this question when we see him as faced with a conflict of values: scientific curiosity versus social consequences. Given the virtual certainty that even the undertaking of the inquiry will reinforce some of the most despicable features of our society, the intensity of the presumed moral dilemma depends critically on the scientific significance of the issue that he is choosing to investigate. Even if the scientific significance were immense, we should certainly question the seriousness of the dilemma, given the likely social consequences. But if the scientific interest of any possible finding is slight, then the dilemma vanishes.

In fact, it seems that the question of the relation, if any, between race and intelligence has little scientific importance (as it has no social importance, except under the assumptions of a racist society). A possible correlation between mean IQ and skin color is of no greater scientific interest than a correlation between any two other arbitrarily selected traits, say, mean height and color of eyes.

4. See the correspondence in *Atlantic*, November 1971.

The empirical results, whatever they may be, appear to have little bearing on any issue of scientific significance. In the present state of scientific understanding, there would appear to be little scientific interest in the discovery that one partly heritable trait correlates (or not) with another partly heritable trait. Such questions might be interesting if the results had some bearing, say, on hypotheses about the physiological mechanisms involved, but this is not the case. Therefore, the investigation seems of quite limited scientific interest, and the zeal and intensity with which some pursue or welcome it cannot reasonably be attributed to a dispassionate desire to advance science. It would, of course, be foolish to claim in response that "society should not be left in ignorance." Society is happily "in ignorance" of insignificant matters of all sorts. And with the best of will it is difficult to avoid questioning the good faith of those who deplore the alleged "anti-intellectualism" of the critics of scientifically trivial and socially malicious investigations. On the contrary, the investigator of race and intelligence might do well to explain the intellectual significance of the topic he is studying and thus enlighten us as to the moral dilemma he perceives. If he perceives none, the conclusion is obvious, with no further discussion.

As to social importance, a correlation between race and mean IQ (were this shown to exist) entails no social consequences except in a racist society in which each individual is assigned to a racial category and dealt with not as an individual in his own right, but as a representative of this category. Herrnstein mentions a possible correlation between height and IQ. Of what social importance is that? None, of course, since our society does not suffer under discrimination by height. We do not insist on assigning each adult to the category "below six feet in height" or "above six feet in height" when we ask what sort of education he should receive or where he should live or what he should do. Rather he is what he is, quite

independent of the mean IQ of people of his height category. In a nonracist society the category of race would be
of no greater significance. The mean IQ of individuals of
a certain racial background is irrelevant to the situation
of a particular individual, who is what he is. Recognizing
this perfectly obvious fact, we are left with little, if any,
plausible justification for an interest in the relation between mean IQ and race, apart from the "justification"
provided by the existence of racial discrimination.

The question of heritability of IQ might conceivably
have some social importance, say, with regard to educational practice. However, even this seems dubious, and
one would like to see an argument. It is, incidentally,
surprising to me that so many commentators should find
it disturbing that IQ might be heritable, perhaps largely
so.* Would it also be disturbing to discover that relative
height, or musical talent, or rank in running the 100 yard
dash is in part genetically determined? Why should one
have preconceptions one way or another about these
questions, and how do the answers to them, whatever
they may be, relate either to serious scientific issues (in
the present state of our knowledge) or to social practice
in a decent society?

---

*An advertisement in the *Harvard Crimson* (November 29,
1971), signed by many faculty members, refers to the "disturbing conclusion that 'intelligence' is largely genetic, so that over
many, many years society might evolve into classes marked by
distinctly different levels of ability." Since the conclusion does
not follow from the premise, as already noted, it may be that
what disturbs the signers is the "conclusion that 'intelligence' is
largely genetic." Why this should seem disturbing remains ob-
scure.

Psychology's White Face

ROSS A. EVANS

Whatever the pros and cons of separate black studies in the university, the controversy over their desirability, necessity, and indeed their legitimacy has served an important function for the black professional in academe. As a black psychologist I, like many others, have always tried very hard to treat the development of my professional proficiency apart from my personal experience as a black American. In so doing, I find now that I have allowed myself to be diverted from the essentially racist elements buried in many of the fundamental assumptions of American psychology, assumptions which have served to punish black Americans brutally with the sanction and participation of too many black as well as white psychologists.

If we, as we rarely do, consider that one of the objectives of training in psychology is to enable the student to transcend his culture, then we have no choice but to view psychology's success in this area with extreme skepticism; for those of us who are products of the psychology taught in colleges and universities must recognize that most undergraduate curricula in psychology are dangerously culture bound. And let's face it—American culture is bound by racism. On reflection, it seems naïve ever to have

SOURCE: Ross A. Evans, "Psychology's White Face," *Social Policy* 1, no. 6 (March-April 1971).

supposed that American psychology managed to escape the pernicious effects of racism, which have permeated every other facet of American life. And yet we assumed precisely that.

Things are beginning to change now. In response to greater militancy inside various segments of black America, and to the professional dissatisfaction voiced in various academic caucuses, black psychologists have organized themselves and have begun to try to break out of the lockstep in which their professional identity and their discipline have been caught.

THE INFERIORITY ASSUMPTION

The major deficiencies in academic psychology as they relate to the black experience may be subsumed under what might be termed the "inferiority assumption"—an assumption that has led to a general inferiority orientation of psychologists toward black people. Modern American psychology, at its inception around the turn of the century, tended largely to ignore the real problems confronting the black American and chose rather to concentrate its efforts on pursuing "scientific" explanations of an inferiority that was *assumed*. My purpose here is not to indict the psychologist of that day for making that assumption, but rather to consider the continuing effects of that assumption on the course of scholarly inquiry into questions relevant to the black condition.

The selective application of the inferiority assumption has been so thoroughly and subtly incorporated into the academic style of American psychology that it hardly appears to exist at all. For example, take the question of intelligence-testing. The two most commonly used individual intelligence scales for children were initially constructed, pretested, and standardized with a native-born white reference population.* Nonwhite and foreign-born children were excluded from the item selection and standardization samples on the assumption that their inclusion would make the standardization norms unduly low and nonpredictive for children from the majority culture. But it is with revealing irony that one further observes that these very tests are currently being used to consign minority children to classes for the mentally retarded or to the lowest educational tracks in the public schools. Moreover, data from these instruments provide sanction for the increasingly numerous statements (issued so casually by many professionals, including psychologists) that inform the lay public that 50 percent of the school children in this or that black community are mentally retarded. But what is even more disturbing than these assertions themselves is the professional reaction to them. For the historically conditioned professional, the response has typically been the initiation of frantic activities directed toward discovering the causes of the assumed inferiority, rather than critical reevaluation of the measuring instruments themselves.

Two examples from the history of American psychometry make the significance and overtness of inferiority assumptions perfectly clear.

During World War I, the United States Armed Forces undertook a massive psychological testing program in an effort to identify those who were intellectually unsuitable for military conscription. The results of that testing program, inadequate as it was, revealed several dramatic differences as a function of race, socioeconomic status, and

---

*The scales to which I refer are the Stanford-Binet Intelligence Test and the Wechsler Intelligence Scale for Children. It should be noted that the Wechsler Scale was constructed in 1955 and has never been revised. The Stanford-Binet, which has undergone two major revisions—the latest published in 1960—has not to date corrected this deficiency.

geographic location: whites tended to score higher than blacks; Northern whites scored higher than Southern whites; Northern blacks performed better than Southern blacks; the scores of those in higher socioeconomic brackets were superior to those of their lower socioeconomic counterparts; and so forth. These results have been well publicized, and are not of major importance here. What is of interest is the fact that 50 percent of the *white* draftees failed to achieve a mental age of thirteen years—an achievement level that was being proposed as a cutoff point for feeblemindedness. This finding, suggesting that half the draft-age white American males were feebleminded, understandably created tremendous controversy and disquietude. However, as recent students have pointed out, a saner view followed the alarms: " . . . both psychologists and the public at large soon realized that any definition of feeblemindedness that classifies 50 percent of the population as feebleminded must be suspect to say the least." One wonders when a saner view will set in with respect to figures on the prevalence of mental retardation among children from low-income *black* communities.

A second example from the field of psychometry, in which the inferiority assumption is conspicuously absent, concerns the question of sex differences in intelligence. Consider the following excerpts from Anne Anastasi's *Psychological Testing* (1961) on the construction of the 1937 revision of the Stanford-Binet:

In the final selection of items, consideration was not only given to age differentiation and internal consistency, but also the reduction and balancing of sex differences in percentage passing of either sex, on the *assumption* that such items might reflect purely fortuitous and irrelevant differences in the experiences of the two sexes. [Italics mine.—R.E.]

And later:

For proper interpretation of test scores, the test user should be aware of such item selection procedures. A statement that boys and girls do not differ significantly in Stanford-Binet IQ, for example, provides no information whatever regarding sex differences in intelligence. Since sex differences were deliberately eliminated in the process of selecting items for the test, their absence from the final score merely indicates that this aspect of test construction was successfully executed.

In essence, what the above excerpts indicate is that the test constructors assumed a priori that there should be no sex differences in intelligence; therefore they developed an instrument that precluded them. On the contrary, these same test constructors assumed a priori that there should be racial differences in intelligence (favoring whites). Thus it should not be surprising, in my opinion, that this result has generally obtained.

It is true that some effort has been made toward the development of so-called "culture-fair" tests; but the general consensus has been that these instruments have little practical utility since they do not correlate highly with the indicators of success (typically, school achievement) within the majority culture. However, I believe that the question must be raised as to whether a "culture-fair" test logically should be expected to predict success in a society that is decidedly *unfair*—including, of course, the educational system itself. The relatively high correlation between the more culture-bound tests and such measures as school achievement may, in fact, be simply a statistical artifact reflecting the ubiquitous effects of cultural and racial biases in American society. The ramifications of this likely state of affairs are far-reaching: On the one hand, psychologists are able to justify their continued use of admittedly biased measurement devices on the basis of empirical predictive validity; on the other hand, educators are able to rationalize their failure to teach black children on the basis of the learners' inferior intellectual potential. Thus two related aspects of a biased system achieve equilibrium through the process of reciprocal reinforcement.

THE PATHOLOGY MODEL

Another manifestation of the inferiority assumption in American psychology appears in its pathology orientation toward the collective adjustment problems and adjustment processes of black people. That is to say, American psychologists, in their effort to interpret behavioral and personality differences between whites and blacks, have attempted to apply psychological constructs based on *within-group* deviations from white middle-class standards to differences occurring *between* the two groups. Thus, for example, "hypersensitive" behavior on the part of black people as a group becomes theoretically equivalent to ostensibly similar behavior occurring in a white psychiatric patient.

The most glaring fallacy here is that one logically cannot apply clinical models based on individual deviations from a cultural norm to groups of individuals with different cultural experiences and standards. Moreover, one should not even attempt to extrapolate from such models without first taking into account the situational validity of the constructs involved. To be more concrete, if one is to infer that "hypersensitivity" without realistic provocation is indicative of a pathological condition, then one must establish the absence of such provocation in the situation under consideration. In the present example, this would raise the question whether "hypersensitivity" on the part of black people is, in fact, unrealistic, or whether it is actually a logical adaptive reaction to the circumstances of their everyday existence. This issue, I believe, has not been given adequate consideration in pathology-oriented research and theory pertaining to the social adjustment of black people.

The pathology orientation to the situational adjustment problems of black people has also led to concentration on instances of social and/or personal maladjustment of blacks, with only philosophical attention paid to the adverse social and environmental factors that produce them. At the same time, the pathology orientation tends to ignore the positive aspects of adjustment on the part of black people, who face conditions of intense and sustained adversity. The more meaningful question is not why so many black people become maladjusted, but rather why so many of them do not.

I believe important lessons on techniques for overcoming adversity could be learned from the examination of case studies of black people who have managed to neutralize the debilitating and degrading effects of racism and oppression. Why must only negative illustrations be presented in the psychological literature? And, then again, when negative illustrations are presented, why must they be analyzed and interpreted within a pathological rather than a social adaptation framework? It is important to remember that all behavior is legitimate and purposeful, even though some of it is regrettable and/or unsuccessful. Failure, however, should not be equated with pathology. Perhaps an analogy will help to clarify my point.

Consider a situation in which three boys are walking through a cow pasture when suddenly they observe a dangerous bull charging in their direction. All three boys react instantly by racing across the pasture toward a fence beyond which lies safety. Now, as it happens, two of the boys are tall, with long legs, while the third lad is built somewhat closer to the ground. Upon reaching the fence, all three boys attempt to leap over. However, only the two taller youths are successful; the short boy doesn't make it simply because his legs aren't long enough.

Therefore, he scrambles around, avoiding the bull, until he decides to try crawling under the fence. This works, and the boys continue on their way.

An attempt to analyze the behavior of the short youth on the basis of the pathology model might proceed as follows: First of all, the short boy's initial effort to leap over the fence perhaps reflects an unrealistic aspiration resulting from low self-esteem and feelings of self-worthlessness. The fact that he imitates the behavior of the taller boys reveals an internalization of tall-boy standards, indicating a subconscious wish to be tall accompanied by a rejection of all short people, including himself. And so forth. On the other hand, a more parsimonious explanation may simply be that the short boy initially attempted a logical approach to the solution of a problem, and it didn't work. Whether or not he actually did model his behavior after that of the tall boys is irrelevant here, since imitation of successful behavior is certainly a logical strategy. The fact is that the approach didn't solve the problem, and he had to try something different.

The above analogy, I believe, bears directly upon the historical attempts of blacks to overcome the social and economic barriers to full American citizenship. And it also characterizes the typical reaction of psychologists and other social scientists to those attempts. Historically, American social scientists have reacted to the problems of black people in a compartmentalized fashion. The problem of gaining entry into the social and economic mainstream of American life has confronted virtually every minority immigrant group (in varying degrees) since the nation's founding. Yet the similarity between the adaptive reactions to the barriers utilized by the immigrant groups and those attempted by blacks has not been adequately appreciated.

Immigrant minority-group members attempted to modify their physical appearance and social demeanor (e.g., adopting American haircuts, abandoning Old World customs, anglicizing surnames, etc.) in an effort to become more acceptable to Anglo-Americans; this effort was widely regarded as positive adaptive behavior designed to facilitate their assimilation into the American mainstream.* Similarly, black Americans attempted to modify their physical and behavioral characteristics, (e.g., straightening their hair, lightening their skin, talking "proper," etc.), perhaps also to make themselves more like the "real" Americans. However, in this case the behavior was considered pathological, reflecting self-rejection, self-hatred, and the rest. (This is not to suggest that the phenomenon of self-hatred does not exist for some individual black people. However, I do not believe that wholesale generalization of this tendency to black people as a group, or even a substantial percentage of them, is justifiable.) The main point here, however, should not be obscured: for the blacks, the early attempts at acquiring "white folks'" characteristics and mannerisms simply didn't work to their advantage. But is this really any reason to consider these attempts to be reflective of underlying group pathology?

*Let me point out that it is not my contention that immigrant groups were ever assimilated into the American sociocultural fabric, as suggested by the "melting pot" myth. True, the degree of assimilation they did achieve is substantially greater than that attained by black Americans. But the major point here is that both immigrants and blacks did make concerted efforts to decrease the dissimilarity between themselves and the more established Anglo-American. For an insightful exposition of the question regarding the assimilation of immigrants and blacks, the reader is referred to Colin Greer's *Cobweb Attitudes: Essays on Educational and Cultural Mythology* (New York: Teachers College Press, 1970).

A NEW JUSTIFICATION

The inferiority assumption and the pathology model add up, on the liberal side, to compensation. Compensatory education and compensatory intervention in ghetto family life represent what amounts to a cultural deviance approach to black children from low-income families. This approach evaluates the childrearing circumstances in low-income homes in terms of the degree of their deviation from the characteristics of the middle-class milieu, which is taken as an unequivocal standard of excellence in most, if not all, respects.

It is not my contention that the conditions of slum life are optimally conducive to intellectual stimulation and development. Rather, my point is that behavioral researchers have been overly zealous in identifying a multiplicity of childrearing and parent-child interactional differences between middle-income whites and low-income blacks that are automatically assumed to represent deficiencies in the upbringing of black children, regardless of the strengths of that upbringing and the success of individuals sprung from it. I should like to emphasize that what I am referring to are not the obviously handicapping factors associated with slum living, such as overcrowded living conditions, hunger, the absence of the mother in the home because of her need to work, etc. What I am referring to are those relatively subtle, value-related, lifestyle variables whose effect on intellectual and personality development we know so little about. Nevertheless, based on only scanty (and confounded) correlational evidence, researchers and practitioners have begun to propose intervention programs designed to restructure the life-style and parent-child interactional patterns of large masses of low-income black families. Based on the notion of deprivation, programs are built on weaknesses rather than strengths. Most fail; and the failure is blamed on the children involved, not on the program or on the research that preceded it. If compensatory programs don't work, then move in on the home with more of the same assumptions, presumptions, and stereotypes. There is no question that poor, black children do less well in school, but there is by no means such certainty that they do less well because of readily identifiable deficits in their cultural background. Moreover, as L. Alan Stroufe cogently observes, " . . . these proposals have generated no more debate than surrounds a decision to alter the lighting in an experimental rat colony."

Perhaps the most disturbing aspect of this displacement of emphasis from early childhood education to the restructuring of family interactional patterns is that it seems clearly to be an example of buck-passing; and the buck that is being passed is the same one secondary-school educators foisted upon the elementary schools, which, in turn, passed it on to preschool compensatory educational programs. Thus it appears that through this process of educational reductionism, we are gradually working ourselves back toward the point of conception.

The immediate result of this tendency has been the replacement of the concept of genetic inferiority with the concept of environmental inferiority. The justification may be different, but the implications are the same—that black people, on the whole, constitute an inferior breed. But ironically, while geneticists readily admit that they are nowhere close to being able to deal scientifically with the questions of genetic inferiority, psychologists appear to be somewhat less modest. Compensatory educational programs continue to be evaluated; and with every negative finding reported, the concept of irreversible environmental inferiority is reinforced.

As psychologists we must ask ourselves why we continue to employ inadequate instruments to measure expected outcomes of socially important research without

sharing with the public our awareness of these limitations. And as psychologists—black psychologists, in particular—we should state loudly and clearly that even if an
intervention program does produce important behavioral changes, the state of the art of behavioral research
is such that we are not even sure that we could detect
them—especially on a short-term basis. I am not suggesting that we should call a moratorium on important
evaluative educational and social research until we have
more adequate measurement instruments and research
methodologies. What I am suggesting is that we stop
leading the lay public to believe that we are presently
equipped to do a job that we ourselves know we are not.

It is past time for yesterday's black students of psychology (especially black graduate students trained in white
universities) who readily accepted—or failed to challenge
—the fundamentally racist assumptions of their discipline to reject those assumptions. Too many of us have
subordinated the legitimacy of our own black experience
in deference to the arbitrarily determined "objectivity"
of the scientist we wanted to become. It is time that we,
like black Americans in other areas of American life, decide on an alternative strategy, like the boy attempting to
escape the bull. When we do that, it may even be that we
will contribute a new perspective and a new, unique impetus for evaluating both what psychology is and what it
should be.

What Is Intelligence?

JEROME KAGAN

As John Stuart Mill once noted, "The tendency has always been strong to believe that whatever received a name must be an entity of being, having an independent existence of its own. And if no real entity answering to the name could be found, men did not for that reason suppose that none existed, but imagined that it was something peculiarly abstruse and mysterious."

Mill may have been thinking of the enigmatic concept of intelligence when he wrote those words; it has become one of the most controversial and confused words in our lexicon. It was inevitable that many societies would invent the idea of intelligence since man requires an explanation for the obvious differences among persons in their ability to adapt to the problems posed by their environments. Intelligence is the psychic analogue of physical endurance. In those societies where the critical environmental challenges remain relatively constant over time, there is usually social consensus on the characteristics that define a "smart person," although one culture may emphasize risk taking, another activity level, another quality of memory, a fourth the capacity for pensive reflection. Less than 100 years ago, Sir Francis Galton believed that intelligence could be measured by evaluating visual and auditory acuity. His definition has been totally

SOURCE: Jerome Kagan, "What Is Intelligence?" *Social Policy* 4, no. 1 (July-August 1973).

abandoned in favor of size of vocabulary, ability to solve arithmetic problems, and analogical reasoning.

Despite the serious lack of unanimity among both cultures and scientists as to what intelligence is and how it should be assessed, most Americans believe that differences in mental capability—no matter what tests are used—are due in large measure to inherited biological factors. Hence they are not very particular about the quality of the scientific evidence that supports this belief. I do not believe that 80 percent of IQ is inherited, and I want to make my case on both logical and empirical grounds.

The first reason for doubting that differences in IQ are inherited has to do with the test on which the heritability estimates are made. Although scientists (for example, Piaget, Guilford, and others) hold varied conceptions of intelligence, one type of test dominates because school progress became the criterion against which the value of the intelligence test would be judged. Once that decision had been made, and it was made self-consciously by the inventors of the test, the history of the last sixty years was inevitable. Since questions that did not predict progress in reading, arithmetic, and composition were purposely omitted from the intelligence test, it is not surprising that a high IQ score predicts school and college grades. Since satisfactory grades are a major requirement for college admission and subsequent entry into professions that allow the accumulation of status, power, and wealth, it is again necessarily true that the IQ score should predict more successful adaptation in our society. However, the original basis for selecting the test questions has been forgotten. The causal relation between IQ and eventual success has been turned on its head. It is argued that teachers and lawyers have higher intelligence than cab drivers or house painters because they possess biologically better nervous systems, rather than because the circumstances of their rearing familiarized them with the language and class of problems presented on the IQ test and nurtured the motivation to solve those problems.

For example, compare five questions taken from the vocabulary and information tests of the Wechsler Scale and five questions taken from a test devised to be familiar to urban poor blacks; the Wechsler questions, as we know, are familiar to middle-class white Americans.

Wechsler Test
1. Who wrote *Hamlet*?
2. Who wrote the *Iliad*?
3. What is the Koran?
4. What does *audacious* mean?
5. What does *plagiarize* mean?

Dove's Test
1. In C. C. Ryder what does C. C. stand for?
2. What is a gashead?
3. What is Willy Mays's last name?
4. What does "handkerchief head" mean?
5. Whom did "Stagger Lee" kill in the famous blues legend?

It is unreasonable to assume that high scores on either test have anything to do with basic mental capacity. A person's score reflects the probability that he has been exposed to the information requested.

AFRICAN AND LATIN AMERICAN STUDIES

Consider a related example. In Kenya Janet Fjellman worked with a group of children living in a rural area and with an urban group living in Nairobi.[1] The rural adults make a distinction between domestic and wild animals that adults in Nairobi ignore. When the unschooled rural children were asked to sort an array of animal pictures into conceptually similar categories, they divided them on the basis of domestic versus wild; the city children sorted by color. The assumption behind the scoring and interpretation of modern intelligence tests would have

1. Janet Fjellman, "The Myth of Primitive Mentality" (Ph.D. diss., Stanford University, 1971).

classified the city children as nonabstract and by inference less intelligent than the rural children. Since this decision violates our intuitions concerning the nature of intelligence and the role of schools in promoting abstract thought, we are forced to the reasonable interpretation that differential familiarity with the concept "domestic versus wild animal" was responsible for the results achieved by the two groups. This explanation is supported by the fact that the city children produced more abstract categories when geometric shapes like circles and squares were the materials manipulated.

If the Wechsler and Binet Scales were translated into Spanish, Swahili, and Chinese and given to every ten year old in Latin America, East Africa, or China, the majority would obtain IQ scores in the mentally retarded range. It is bizarre to contend that most of the children in the world are mentally retarded with the exception of middle-class Americans and Europeans.

I have recently returned from eight months of work in an isolated Indian village in northwest Guatemala. This village has 850 inhabitants, no electricity, no sanitary facilities, and no easy access to a large city. Translated versions of standard IQ tests would have revealed IQ quotients of fifty or sixty in almost all children. However, we administered tests, in dialect, of recall and recognition memory, perceptual analysis, and perceptual inference to children five through twelve years of age in these villages as well as to children in the United States. Although the five and eight year olds performed less well than the Americans on most tests, there was no cultural difference on any of these tests at ten and eleven years of age.

Our interpretation of this provocative fact is that an executive cognitive process that is maturationally monitored emerges in all children sometime between five and ten years. It can emerge as early as age five in very favorable environments, but as late as age ten in unfavorable ones. Guatemalan children, who are frequently ill and

live in restricted and homogeneous environments, develop this important competence more slowly than
Americans. But they continue to grow and by age eleven
are comparable to middle-class American children in
basic intellectual competences, such as memory, inference, perceptual analysis, and reasoning. They are intelligent, even though their IQ scores are low because of the
obvious cultural bias in the test.

It is interesting to note that the difference between the
Guatemalan and American children in rate of emergence
of the cognitive executive is very much like the difference
between poor and middle-class children in American cit-
ies. Working in Grand Rapids, J. Bosco has found that
there is an enormous difference in the ability to mobilize
executive processes for a difficult perceptual detection
task between lower-class and middle-class five and eight
year olds, but no difference between lower-class and middle-class eleven year olds.[2] Thus, as with the Guatemalan
children, poor American children are also slower in attaining the basic cognitive competence. However, being
slower is not the same as having qualitatively different
competence.

It may be helpful to pose an analogy involving physical
maturation. Some children reach physiological puberty at
age ten, others at age fifteen, *but all reach puberty.* If educators and citizens behaved toward this developmental phenomenon the way they do toward cognitive talents like IQ
or achievement tests, we would treat all thirteen year olds
who had not reached menarche or had no pubic hair as
qualitatively different from those that had and assume
that they were destined never to attain fertility.

2. James Bosco, "The Visual Information Processing Speed of
Lower and Middle Class Children," *Child Development* 43 (1972):
1418–1422.

THE GENETIC FALLACY

If this conclusion has intuitive appeal, why do many well-read, thinking people believe that 80 percent of the variation in intelligence is inherited? There seem to be two reasons for this view. Since the genetic differences among humans probably influence some aspects of mental functioning, it seems like such a small leap to the stronger statement that differences in intelligence are primarily genetic in origin. However true the first statement, the second does not necessarily follow. Heredity also controls the amount and distribution of the hair on our heads, but the distribution of facial hair in Harvard Square is primarily attributable to cultural mores, not to biology.

Hence the more serious basis for the genetic argument is the undeniable fact that the closer the genetic relation between two people, the more similar their IQ scores. Since this fact is the principal rational support for the conclusion that a person's IQ is 80 percent heredity, we must examine the bases for that fact to see if this inference is reasonable.

Scientists assume that the *critical* test of the genetic hypothesis is contained in comparisons of the IQ scores of identical and nonidentical twins reared in the same or different environments. It is true that the IQs of identical twins, who have the same set of genes, are more similar than those of nonidentical twins, who have a different genetic structure. However, Dr. Richard Smith, who compared ninety pairs of identical twins and seventy-four pairs of nonidentical twins, found that the identical twins, especially females, were also more similar in behaviors that are likely to be the result of similar experience, not heredity.[3] For example, identical twins were more likely

3. Richard T. Smith, "A Comparison of Socioenvironmental

to study and do their homework together, to have the same set of very close friends, and to have similar food preferences. Smith concluded:

> there is a difference in the overall environment of the two types of twins which will, in turn, influence intrapair differences. . . . It seems evident that the assumption of a common environment for monozygotic and dizygotic twins is of doubtful validity and, therefore, the role of environment needs to be more fully evaluated in twin studies.

However, since the IQs of identical twins reared in different environments are also more similar than those of people selected at random, the role of heredity seems certain and the role of environment ambiguous. *But that conclusion requires a condition that is rarely met: namely, that the twins be reared in different home environments and encounter radically different values and treatments.* Since officials responsible for placing children in foster homes try to place them in similar settings, it is likely that most of the twin pairs were sent to families of similar religious, linguistic, racial, and social class background and as a result were exposed to similar experiences.

There are four major studies of identical twins reared in different homes. Cyril Burt reported information on the families to which the twin pairs were sent.[4] Forty-one percent of the twin pairs grew up in homes that were highly similar socioeconomically; only 26 percent (twelve twin pairs) were sent to families markedly different in social class. In nine of these twelve pairs the twin who lived in the upper-middle-class home had a higher IQ

Factors in Monozygotic and Dizygotic Twins: Testing an Assumption," in *Methods and Goals in Human Behavior Genetics*, ed. S. G. Vandenberg (New York: Academic Press, 1965), pp. 45–61.

4. Cyril Burt, "The Genetic Determination of Differences in Intelligence: A Study of Monozygotic Twins Reared Together and Apart," *British Journal of Psychology* 57 (1966): 137–153.

than the twin adopted by the working-class home.

In an earlier study only four of nineteen pairs of separated twins (21 percent) grew up in homes with large differences in educational attainment. Let us see what happened to these children. In one pair one girl had five years of schooling while her sister had three years of college. In two pairs one finished high school, the other the eighth grade. In the most dramatic pair one sister with an IQ of ninety-two only finished third grade; the other with an IQ of 116 had a college degree. Now it is less clear that the similarity in IQ scores between identical twins reared apart is primarily a result of common heredity.

ENVIRONMENTAL PRESS

Robert McCall of the Fels Research Institute has found that the correlation between pairs of genetically unrelated white children from the same social class is not 0.0, but 0.3. Since the correlation between brothers and sisters living in the same home is only 0.5, it is reasonable to suggest that the similarity in IQ scores between siblings or separated twins should not be interpreted as primarily genetic in origin. We have recently analyzed some data that provide additional support for this view.

The data were supplied by Drs. Janet Hardy and Doris Welcher of the Johns Hopkins Child Growth and Development Study. They selected a random sample of over 400 children from their records, all of whom had been administered a Wechsler IQ test when they were about seven years old. Most of the children were from poor black families residing in a relatively homogeneous ghetto environment. When pairs of black children were selected at random, the correlation between their IQ scores was low and the average difference in their IQs a little over twelve points. However, when pairs of children were selected so that each pair was of the same sex and their mothers of similar age and years of education, the average difference in IQ dropped to nine points, which is only a little larger than the average difference of seven points reported for the 122 pairs of identical twins reared in different homes, and smaller than the average difference of fourteen points found for one set of twins when IQ equivalents for their scores were computed. More specifically, among the genetically unrelated pairs of children matched only on maternal age and education, 43 percent had IQ differences of six points or less. This degree of similarity approaches that found for two of the studies of separated identical twins, where the comparable proportions were 47 and 50 percent. Since matching genetically unrelated children on only maternal age and schooling markedly increased the similarity of their IQs, it is reasonable to argue that the similar IQ scores of separated twins could be the partial result of placement in similar home environments.

Let us assume that number of years in school (which typically varied between seven and twelve years for this ghetto population) reflects primarily the mother's concern with traditional academic accomplishment, rather than her biological ability to do school work. If that motivation were reflected in her treatment of her children, the similarity in IQ for these matched pairs would argue for the profound effect of environment on IQ.

Those who favor the genetic hypothesis reply that social class is correlated with IQ because biologically more intelligent people rise in social class. Hence matching children on their mother's education is equivalent to matching them on basic intelligence. This statement ignores the fact that the first generation of Irish or Italian Catholic and Jewish immigrants who came to America typically did not attain any more formal schooling or higher IQ scores than contemporary blacks, Puerto Ricans, and Mexican-Americans. Today the distribution of

IQ scores of Jews and Catholics is similar to that of the dominant group of white Protestants. Since it is unlikely that the "genes governing intelligence" in these ethnic groups have changed during the last fifty years, it is fair to question the assumption that a low position on the social class ladder at a particular time in history is primarily the result of hereditary factors.

Moreover, if the genetic interpretation of social class differences were correct, we should not see any major class differences in the parental treatment of young children, for the IQ differences between middle-class and lower-class parents and children are presumably the product of internal biological forces, not differential socialization. Any evidence of social class differences in parental treatment that was theoretically concordant with high IQs would weaken the genetic position.

Recent studies have found dramatic differences in the mother's treatment of her child as a function of her education and her husband's occupation; differences that imply that better educated parents create experiences for their children that facilitate their performance on IQ tests.

HERITABILITY RATIO

A third source of vulnerability in the genetic argument centers on the legitimacy of the *heritability ratio* to assess the magnitude of hereditary influence, which is based on differences between populations on a trait. Lorenz has criticized this view: "The formulation that it is not characters but *differences between characters* which may be described as innate is, in my opinion, an unsuccessful attempt to arrive at an operational definition of heritability."

Moreover, M. Nei and A. K. Roychoudhury of Brown University have found that the gene differences among

Caucasian, Japanese, and Negro populations for specific proteins are no greater than those between individuals from the same ethnic group. They suggest:

> It may be concluded that the genes in the three major ethnic groups of man are remarkably similar, although the phenotypic differences in pigmentation and facial structure are conspicuous. It seems likely that the genes controlling these morphological characters were subjected to stronger natural selection than average genes in the process of racial differentiation. . . . The differences between these ethnic groups are of the same order of magnitude as those between local populations of the house mouse.[5]

Estimates of the heritability ratio for IQ are usually based on the difference in the IQ correlation between identical and nonidentical twins. The ratio is based on the assumption that the causes of variation in IQ can be added together, some due to environment and some due to heredity. A serious criticism of the use of the heritability ratio is that its proponents have ignored the possibility that heredity and environment might be highly correlated and assume the ratio to be zero. There is good reason to believe that aspects of the young child's temperament are treated differently by middle-class and lower-class parents; as a result the qualities measured by IQ tests are enhanced in middle-class homes and perhaps suppressed in working-class homes. If this were true, current heritability values might be spuriously high.

Consider a concrete illustration of this issue. I recently completed a longitudinal study of a large group of firstborn white children who were followed from four through twenty-seven months of age.[6] There was a major

5. M. Nei and A. K. Roychoudhury, "Gene Differences Between Caucasian, Negro and Japanese Populations," *Science* 177 (1972): 434–435.
6. Jerome Kagan, *Change and Continuity in Infancy* (New York: John Wiley, 1971).

difference among the four month olds in the tendency to babble spontaneously—some infants were extremely quiet while others were continuously cooing. Let us assume that biological factors are partially responsible for this variation in infant "vocalization." Observations in the homes of these children revealed that college-educated mothers were much more responsive to their infants' babbling than mothers with less than a high school education. The middle-class mothers talked back to their infants and long reciprocal dialogues ensued. At twenty-seven months the girls who were the most talkative and had the largest vocabularies (and by inference high IQ scores) had been highly vocal infants reared by college-educated mothers. Highly vocal infants raised by lower-middle-class mothers were significantly less proficient verbally.

Since social class is typically correlated with IQ score it is reasonable to suggest that the heritability values, which are interpreted as reflecting genetic factors, are spuriously inflated to an unknown degree by a *strong relation* between particular temperamental traits and social class differences in parental responsivity to these traits. Arthur Jensen assumes this correlation is zero when he computes his heritability ratios.[7]

There are, therefore, three bases for doubting the provocative statement that heredity accounts for most of the variation in IQ score: (1) the IQ test is a culturally biased instrument; (2) the similar IQ scores of genetically related people can be duplicated in genetically unrelated people who live in similar environments; and (3) the probable correlation between heredity and environment is ignored in current interpretations of the heritability ratio.

7. Arthur R. Jensen, "How Much Can We Boost IQ and Scholastic Achievement," *Harvard Educational Review* 39 (1969): 1–123.

IQ FOR SOCIAL HIERARCHY

Why, then, do many scientists and parents continue to believe in the 80 percent figure for the heritability of IQ, excluding the small proportion of children—3 percent at most—with specific forms of severe mental retardation due to known genetic factors. Perhaps one reason is that every society believes that in order to maintain stability a small group must possess some power over the much larger citizenry. In most instances the psychological traits of those in power become, with time, the explanation for the differences in status and privilege. Tenth-century Europe awarded power to those who were assumed to be more religious than their brothers. The presumption of a capacity for more intense religiosity provided a rationale that allowed the larger society to accept that a privileged few were permitted entry into marble halls. In the isolated Mayan Indian village in which I worked, the men told us that women must never be given responsibility because they are born fearful and cannot make decisions. Being born male is the village's explanation of differential ability to wield power. Contemporary American society explains its unequal distribution of status as a product of differential intelligence, rather than innate religiosity or sex, and it makes the same genetic arguments. Intelligence is America's modern interpretation of saintliness, religiosity, courage, or moral intensity, and it has become the basis for the awarding of prizes.

The American preference for explaining differences in success as a function of heredity is analogous to the view of many local community developers in Guatemala that they are due to malnutrition. In the village in which I worked there was a stout, jovial young Guatemalan, whom I shall call Sebastian, who was spending thirty months organizing cooperative ventures among the resistant Indians. He became visibly upset when I suggested that the quality of nutrition influenced the health, size, and feelings of well-being of the Indians but probably had minimal influence on their basic intellectual capacities. His usually soft and smiling face hardened when he realized that each of us held such polarized opinions on this issue. Since the scientific evidence is equivocal, it is of interest to consider why he felt so strongly.

During each significant era of civilization an individual's prestige, dignity, and access to signs of power are facilitated by the possession of a small collection of symbolic attributes that, depending on place and period, can be inherited, acquired, or seized. The small band of devoted people who devote part of their lives to aiding the disenfranchised wish to maximize the latter's access to these valued psychological resources. There is an implicit recognition of the fact that all people require a belief in their essential "goodness." If we were to ask a poor Indian in San Marcos, a black in Chicago, or a Mexican-American in Los Angeles to choose between six less colds a year or the wispy feeling of equality with the members of his community, is there any doubt about his choice? Despite man's attraction to sensory well-being, meat and freedom from cramps are not his first choices if the possibility of enhancing conception of self is the alternative.

Sebastian is faced with a village of undernourished Indians whose inadequate diet makes them dangerously vulnerable to pneumonia, tuberculosis, and a myriad of exotic viruses. An improved diet would probably put several inches and twenty pounds on the average inhabitant and cut his 150 wearisome days of illness by more than half. Unfortunately better health is not enough in modern Central America, where being taller and less feverish do not automatically move an Indian closer to psychological equality. In contemporary Guatemala, as in most of the modernized or modernizing world, the most efficient way for the disenfranchised Indian to gain dignity and power is to become educated and gain the technical skills the larger society is willing to purchase. The Indians have not moved noticeably closer to that goal in the last century. There are three explanations of their inertia—deficiencies in genetics, motivation, or diet.

The first explanation is too pessimistic for Sebastian and the second too difficult to understand. Hence the third is favored for reasons that can best be described as the delusions of the activist. Given any social problem with more than one potential cause, there is usually one salutary action that is the easiest to implement. Since the activist is impatient when there is acute distress to alleviate, he is anxious to do what can be done now, and he experiences an irresistible temptation to construct a simple theory that renders this action logical. Sebastian does not know how to change motivation, and he is not a genetic engineer. But he does know how to persuade the leaders of the community, government officials, and philanthropists to give money and technical aid to increase the village food supply. Therefore, this solution will be rationalized as the cure for the village's plight, which, in the case of San Marcos, is the inability of the Ladino teacher to educate quiet, passive, resistant Indian children. Sebastian's insistence that malnutrition must be the major cause of uneducability quickly becomes synonymous with the statement that malnutrition leads to impaired intelligence.

The Sebastians of the world are not satisfied with working to increase the food supply merely to improve village health. They must also hold the hope that the food will bring educability and access to a more vital participation in the prizes of the larger community. Sebastian must believe that more protein means enhanced status in Guatemalan society. In San Marcos, as in seventeenth-century Massachusetts, grammar and rhetoric have replaced strength, hunting ability, kinship, and physical attractiveness as the attributes that permit ascent in the social structure.

Cultures invent a prize to chase, set rules of pursuit, and award the players different initial handicaps. The expedient theories that society's priests invent regarding the moves a player should make when he is stalled in the game—not unlike being "in jail" in Monopoly—can be superstitions with the thinnest cover of rationality, a kind of counterfeit "Get out of jail free" card.

INTELLIGENCE—AN INVALID CONCEPT

I suggest that the empirical evidence for Sebastian's belief that poor diet is the basic cause of uneducability is as equivocal as the evidence for Jensen's belief that poor genes are the cause. Future research may reveal that heredity makes a major contribution to the different profiles of human talent. But available knowledge is simply too faulty to permit any firm conclusion.

Those who must have an answer to this question will have to be more patient. When I was a student Down's syndrome, which was then called Mongolism, was regarded as nongenetic. We now know that this defect is caused by a chromosomal anomaly. Nature is an elusive teacher, and we must not allow what we may want to believe to interfere with a clear understanding of the messages she has supplied us up to now.

My own belief is that the concept of intelligence is theoretically misleading. For it we should substitute a view in which we delineate basic cognitive processes (like memory and inference) from acquired knowledge. Second, we must recognize that the honing of competence and the filling of a reservoir of knowledge for a particular population are totally dependent on the demands that the children's culture makes of them and their opportunity to perfect their talents. In short, we must view intellectual capability through relativistic lenses.

The Guatemalan child I described earlier knows less than the American child about planes, computers, and fractions. However, he knows much more about how to make rope and tortillas, how to tell the weather from cloud formations, and how to burn an old milpa for the June planting. The American middle-class child knows how to play chess and Scrabble, while the poor ghetto child knows how to play the "dozens" and dupe teachers and police. Each knows what is necessary for his life space. There are only a few dumb children in the world if you classify them from the perspective of the community of adaptation, but millions of dumb children if you classify them from the perspective of another society.

Intro to Herrnstein 101

GEORGE PURVIN

For the past six months I have been nursing some feelings that were bruised in the campus skirmish that took place here at Harvard over Professor Richard Herrnstein's article, "IQ." Before another layer of scar tissue covers my wounds and my memory of the events, I want to write down the reasons why I believe social scientists and psychologists in particular have given a bad account of themselves in this "Herrnstein Affair." Apart from the personal satisfaction that will come from responding to those who hurt my feelings, I hope that widespread discussion of the issues involved will lead psychologists, with or without public prodding, to establish for themselves a code of conduct that will discourage colleagues tempted to follow and broaden the paths of irresponsible research now trod by such psychologists as Jensen, Herrnstein, and Eysenck.

Even as I write these words, I brace myself for the attack that invariably comes from those who interpret the previous statement as an undisguised assault on academic freedom. From those who take this view I ask that judgment be withheld until I have a chance to make my case. To those who feel that my bias against Dr. Herrnstein makes my account of the events of the fall semester of 1971 unreliable, I admit my bias but I believe that as

SOURCE: George Puruin, "Intro to Herrnstein 101," *Social Policy* 4, no. 1 (July-August 1973).

a student in Dr. Herrnstein's class in psychology and one who was involved in most aspects of the polemic I am able to report the events as they occurred in such a way that actual fact and personal bias are clearly distinguishable.

The chronology can wait until those who are unfamiliar with Dr. Herrnstein's article or only vaguely recall it can be brought up to date. The article was published in the September 1971 issue of the *Atlantic Monthly* at a time when it was accurate to identify the author as chairman of the Department of Psychology at Harvard University. The public, of course, unaware that the position of chairman rotates among the professors of psychology at Harvard, would understandably be impressed by the title and would erroneously assume that Dr. Herrnstein has some special qualifications in psychology entitling him to the post.

The editors of the *Atlantic Monthly* set the stage for Herrnstein's article with a long preface, reviewing the Coleman and Moynihan reports, which, as they put it, "grappled with the idea that something within the black community itself was holding back its economic and educational advance." In 1969 the intrepid Dr. Jensen of Berkeley "faced head-on the possibility that blacks and whites differ in inherited intelligence." The editors then comment on the outcry and protest that followed Jensen's article, published first in the *Harvard Educational Review*. They characterized this response as an unjustifiable attempt to limit public discussion of "important, albeit painful social issues." They conclude with the comment that "social legislation must come to terms with actual human potentialities," a viewpoint which in my opinion takes hypotheses on human intelligence out of the laboratories of psychological research and delivers them to legislative chambers for translation into policy which profoundly affects the lives of men, women and especially little children.

Dr. Herrnstein builds his article around a syllogism set

down in bold type under the title of the article and offered as a true or false examination.

1. If differences in mental abilities are inherited, and
2. If success requires those abilities, and
3. If earnings and prestige depend on success,
4. Then social standing will be based to some extent on inherited differences among people.
              TRUE ☐   FALSE ☐

In support of the syllogism, Herrnstein first attempts
to establish that the IQ test is in fact a valid measure of
human intelligence. He surveys the history of intelligence
testing, reviews the work of Alfred Binet, Lewis Terman,
and others, and then concludes with the statement:

The measurement of intelligence is psychology's most
telling accomplishment to date. Without intending to be-
little other psychological ventures, it may be fairly said
that nowhere else—not in psychotherapy, educational reform or consumer research—has there arisen so potent
an instrument as the objective measure of intelligence.

With this "objective measure of intelligence" in hand,
the author turns his attention to the second and third
premise of the syllogism, that IQ or intelligence is related
to occupation, and that occupation is related to social
status. If these two statements are true, then it follows, of
course, that intelligence is related to status.

For evidence he draws on the data of T. W. and M. S.
Harrel, whose 1945 study, published in *Educational and
Psychological Measurement,* suggested that occupations and
the mean IQ of those working in these occupations are
highly correlated. The Harrels ranked seventy-four occupations on the basis of the mean IQ: accountants head the
list with an IQ of 128.1, and teamsters are on the bottom
with 87.7. Dr. Herrnstein ranks sixteen of the seventy-
four occupations; he concludes that not only is there a
relationship between IQ and occupation and social
status, but that these ties make "practical sense" in that

it is the way in which "society expresses its recognition, however imprecise, of the importance and scarcity of intellectual ability."

Dr. Herrnstein must now convince his reader that differences in mental ability are inherited. Here Herrnstein lifts the conclusions of Dr. Jensen, who used data derived from four different studies of identical twins reared apart. Jensen's conclusion, which Herrnstein now reaffirms in support of his syllogism, is that the uncommon similarity in the IQ of these twins reveals that 80 percent of an individual's intelligence is inherited.

Early in his article Herrnstein offers the opinion that we are moving in the direction of a "meritocracy," which he defines as "the advancement of people on the basis of ability, either potential or fulfilled, measured objectively." Now he reasons, since mental ability is for the most part inherited, and since mental ability determines occupation and occupation determines social status, like it or not, as we become a meritocracy:

. . . there will be precipitated out of the mass of humanity a low-capacity (intellectual or otherwise) residue that may be unable to master the common occupations, cannot compete for success and achievement, and are most likely to be born to parents who have similarly failed.

He concludes that "in times to come, as technology advances, the tendency to be unemployed may run in the genes of a family about as certainly as bad teeth do now."

This then is the article that precipitated the polemic, in which I maintain that psychologists have behaved badly. Just a little autobiography is necessary here. After eight years of teaching history and social studies in a public high school as a second career, I began to experience some nagging doubts about a system that inflicts long-term punishment on so many young people.

I refer to the kids who are "not good in school" and yet must show up every day, shuffle from one room to another at the sound of the bell, and fail or do badly in one examination after another. Literally speaking, what a hell of a way to spend ten or more years of life. Apart from the personal discomfort involved, what other problems of contemporary society might be rooted in the fact that large numbers of adults experienced at least ten formative years of life under exactly these circumstances?

My preoccupation with "being smart or dumb in school" led me to the literature on the origins of intelligence, which fairly well convinced me that whatever is operating here is profoundly related to the experience and environment ingested years before induction into formal schooling. I found it difficult to understand why those who hold positions of leadership in education are content to leave those first five years, when intellectual foundations are established, largely to chance. I wrote letters to some of the state education departments, several universities, and some individuals to find out what programs, if any, existed for providing the preschool experience that would properly prepare a child for formal schooling. My inquiries led to an appointment with Burton L. White of Harvard's Laboratory of Human Development, director of Harvard's Preschool Project, and director of the Brookline Early Education Project. Dr. White helped by giving me a position on the staff of the Brookline Early Education Project and recommended me for admission to Harvard Graduate School for Education. I took a leave of absence from Manhasset High School on Long Island and moved to Boston.

In making my selection of courses, it turned out that among all the courses I had taken in getting a bachelor's and a previous master's degree, there was no record of a basic course in psychology. Since all courses in human development presume an undergraduate course in psychology, I decided to repair the deficiency by signing up for Harvard's only course in Introduction to Psychology, "Soc. Sci. 15," pronounced "Sock Sigh," taught jointly by Roger Brown and Richard Herrnstein.

"SOCK SIGH 15"

A week later I took my seat in the Alston Burr lecture hall among more than 300 men and women, each and every one young enough to be my son or daughter. I felt uncomfortable, not entirely because of the discrepancy in years, but because quite frankly I was in awe of my classmates. Each year the guidance department of the school in which I teach, and I assume guidance counselors in most middle-class secondary schools in the country, engage in the mad scramble to get the seniors into college. It is a proud day and a crimson feather in the caps of student, parent, teacher, counselor, and the entire administration when a Harvard acceptance comes through. My recollection of students of mine, who were admitted to Harvard perhaps one every two years, includes memories of the finest, most talented, eager, and able kids you would ever want to meet. Here I was with 300 of them, all in the same place and the same time, doing the same homework and taking the same examinations. I thought back to my own undistinguished high school record and resolved to make up in hard study what I might lack in intellectual equipment (inherited or otherwise) to keep up with my classmates.

With Dr. Herrnstein's assignment sheet in hand, I hurried to the third floor of the Harvard Coop to buy the books and articles I would need to meet the requirements of the course, among which was a reprint of the article by Professor Herrnstein in the previous month's issue of the *Atlantic Monthly*. My initial reaction to the article was disbelief. When I taught American history to high school juniors, we talked about Social Darwinism as something out of the dark past, and I handled the doctrine much the same, I suspect, as my colleagues in the biology department treated the doctrine of spontaneous generation.

Indeed Dr. Herrnstein's basic proposition that social status is pretty well determined the moment the winning sperm makes contact with the egg would, I thought, get the same reception from social scientists as a resurrection of the proposition that a stick buried in the mud would turn into a snake would get from biologists.

I am not sure what I expected to happen that October morning as I crossed the Yard to attend my first lecture that would deal with the unit of intelligence. I knew that the building in which we would meet every Monday and Wednesday at 10:00 A.M. was just a short block from William James Hall, a white stone structure inhabited by many of the world's most famous names in psychology. Surely these giants of the academic community would recognize the words and music of the Herrnstein article as a new version of the old nineteenth-century tune "Social Darwinism in America." I braced myself for the explosion that would surely take place as Herrnstein was called to account for his mischief-making. Part of my present sense of chagrin comes from the fact that I still feel like a damn fool, standing there with my fingers in my ears, waiting for my Harvard heroes to come charging down from their crimson cloud. Not only were there no big academic guns but also no statement, not even a little mild one, like:

Dick, this thing is awfully big with political implications. With a questionable instrument for measurement, such as Stanford-Binet and those "lumped together" twin studies as evidence, you shouldn't have done it.

But all was quiet on campus and in the lecture hall that first week of actual classes. Roger Brown gave the first lecture and led us over the background of intelligence testing. Dr. Herrnstein picked up the theme the following session, putting considerable emphasis, as my notes tell me, on "a universal intellectual capacity," identified by the English army officer and Boer War veteran, Charles

Spearman, which he called the "g" factor.

Reaction to the article and the lecture was soon to come. As we arrived for the third lecture, three or four members of the SDS (Students for a Democratic Society) and the UAG (United Action Group) stood at the entrance to the hall and handed out mimeographed leaflets denouncing Herrnstein as a racist and demanding his dismissal from Harvard. They or other members of the group had managed to get into the hall and affix hand-lettered signs on either side of the chalkboard and on the side walls, repeating the denunciations contained in the leaflets. This was the only occasion, as I recall, that the lecture hall was so decorated, but it marked the beginning of a campaign by the radical groups on campus to call attention to the political implications of the article and to demand that Herrnstein be dismissed.

In December Herrnstein was to tell the *Boston Globe* that he found this activity disruptive to his class. If he was disconcerted, he certainly did not let it interfere with his lectures, which were devoted entirely, my notebook tells me, to building his case in support of the syllogism offered in his article.

Some weeks later Dr. Brown was to lecture on the psychological phenomenon called "the principle of consistency"; for example, members of the John Birch Society concluded immediately that Lee Harvey Oswald was a communist, and left-wing radicals immediately identified Oswald as a right-wing Texas fascist. My reaction to both Professors Herrnstein and Brown is a good example of this principle. No doubt Dr. Herrnstein gave some good and valuable lectures during the semester, but so great was my antipathy to him that I stopped taking notes when he lectured. If he were to say that it was cold outside, I would think to myself: "not so cold." My reaction to Roger Brown demonstrates still another facet of the principle. People at Harvard whose opinion I value speak well of Dr. Brown, both as a social psychologist and as a person. I found myself going through all kinds of gymnastics, so to speak, seeking out statements and ideas expressed in his lectures and his text that would reveal that Dr. Brown really did not share Herrnstein's view on the nature of human intelligence. I was also influenced by his affable and somewhat diffident manner and by the fact that for the most part he gave interesting lectures. I thought his use of O'Neill's *Long Day's Journey* as a case study for some of the principles of Freudian psychology was especially creative.

But try as I might, I can't quite make Dr. Brown come out as one of the "good guys." As my notes and memory tell me, he was a party to the dissimulation that went on in that class, as both professors disguised their bias with a show of objectivity and led us, in what was for most of us our first course in psychology, to the belief that 80 percent of a person's intelligence, as reliably measured by IQ testing, is fixed at the moment of conception. When it became apparent to me that over 300 Harvard undergraduates—this cream of the American secondary school system, these soon-to-become leaders and makers of public policy—were accepting the Jensen thesis as established fact, I resolved that this sort of "teaching" would not go unchallenged.

HARVARD WAS NEUTRAL

I approached a number of members of the faculty, mostly those in the social sciences, to get their thinking on the Herrnstein article, to call attention to the publicity the article had received from the media, and to suggest that some public response was required from scholars and psychologists, in particular, in opposition to the article. Although I did not find many scientists who shared Herrnstein's view, I did not find any who were disposed to make a public statement to the effect that the IQ article was bad social science, bad scholarship, and extremely mischievous. I have reason to believe that many of Harvard's faculty take this view privately but also feel that public statements of this sort would be "unprofessional."

I level no special charge at psychologists as opposed to doctors, lawyers, or even Indian chiefs, but I do suggest that members of all "professions" need to scrutinize how much of what they call "unprofessional behavior" is in reality an unwritten and unspoken agreement that, crudely put, says: "You don't say anything bad about me in public, and I won't say anything bad about you."

With this response from the academic community my resolution to challenge Dr. Herrnstein began to weaken. How was I to get scholars to step out and challenge a colleague on the basis of his morality, as well as his scholarship, if "the club" would interpret such behavior as unprofessional? The only doors standing ajar were those that led to the meetings and rallies of the campus radicals. To whatever extent the Herrnstein affair can serve as a case study of the campus radical in action, it is worth looking at.

I am aware that attendance at a few meetings, a lunch now and again, and a few one-to-one discussions do not qualify me to speak with authority on the nature of radicalism on the college campus. With this caveat in mind I would say that at Harvard all the campus radicals can be accommodated on the chairs, sofas, and a bit of the floor of the average-sized student lounge. The SDS undergraduates are in their late teens or early twenties, mostly but not entirely white, and about equally divided, it seemed, between men and women. The UAG graduate students and faculty are, of course, older and mostly men. Since the entire membership is so actively involved, it is difficult to pick out specific individuals as leaders. I found Hilary Putnam, a professor of philosophy, to be especially interesting. He teaches classes, attends all meetings and rallies, and stands out in Harvard Square in all kinds of weather, selling a radical newspaper that is printed in both English and Spanish. I have the impression that if Harvard had no such individual on the faculty, they would seek one out. It is their way, I think, of demonstrating a commitment to the Jeffersonian principle of tolerating error of opinion, as long "as reason is left free to oppose it." Needless to say, individuals like Dr. Putnam present little threat to the university. The fire that sometimes makes the campus radical an effective leader of student dissent needs to be fanned by issues that touch the lives, fortunes, and consciences of large groups of young people. These issues are few and far between. Vietnam was such an issue. Herrnstein is not.

My own awareness that most students unexcitedly viewed the Herrnstein article as nothing more than new debate on the old nature-nurture controversy convinced me that Herrnstein would be most vulnerable to an academic and intellectual response. I attended a number of SDS and UAG meetings and urged the group to form committees to read the literature, dissect the *Atlantic* article, and hit Herrnstein where it would hurt him the most: give him, as I put it, a swift kick in his scholarship. As it turned out, the SDS and UAG put out two pieces: "Born to Be Unemployed" and an annotated reprint of the Herrnstein article, both of which developed some first-rate challenges to Herrnstein's scholarship and faulty reasoning. Unfortunately these pieces did little to draw any widespread student support. Some students will literally not read any article or listen to any statement that comes from the SDS. Others, in line with the principle of consistency, read the message and automatically move in support of the other side. There is little that can be done about this population. However, I think it is regrettable that those students who might have supported a movement to identify the parameters of legitimate and responsible research were turned off by SDS literature and speeches, which mixed well-reasoned arguments with unsupportable allegations and inaccurate statements. A number of liberal and uncommitted students told me that they objected to the Herrnstein poster done by the UAG that appeared all over the campus. It had a picture of Dr. Herrnstein under the caption "wanted for racism" and called him "the pigeon man." Dr. Herrnstein has done work in operant conditioning and the reference to the pigeons was an allegation, unsupported as far as I know, that he, like one of the villains out of Batman, had conditioned pigeons to assist the Army in search and destroy missions in Vietnam. A number of students objected to calling Herrnstein a racist. They were quick to point out that, unlike Jensen, Herrnstein avoids discussion of race in connection with intelligence.

I suspect that the rhetoric that most repelled liberal support was the theme repeated over and over again, especially by speakers at rallies, that Richard Herrnstein was merely a pawn in a gigantic plot to prepare the American people for policies and programs designed to reduce certain minority groups, blacks, Puerto Ricans, and Chicanos, in particular, to economic peonage; to so dehumanize this population that the nation would even accept genocide. To the liberal Attica was a Rockefeller blunder; to the campus radical it is another link in the chain of conspiracy that stretches from the Chase Manhattan bank in New York to the "command post" at Harvard. More than the rhetoric repels. As one draws closer to the campus radical, one is aware that real fires of revolution lie smoldering in the minds and passions of these, for the most part, soft-spoken young men and women. I for one get nervous when I think about Thomas Jefferson's quote about watering the tree of liberty with the blood of tyrants, especially when it is not made clear who is going to define the word "tyrant." I get the uneasy feeling that these intense young men and women, soft-spoken or not, would be capable of signing papers that would deliver "tyrants," perhaps me along with Herrnstein, to the guillotine or *la pared.*

On the other hand it needs to be said that the radicals get a bad press and little credit for the important contributions that they make to the academic community, of which they are a part.

As the Harvard *Crimson,* no friend to the SDS, was to bring out in an editorial later that year, the SDS and UAG deserve credit for focusing attention on the Herrnstein article and all of its ramifications. Surely it is a kind of reverse name-calling to dismiss well-reasoned arguments as worthless because they issue from the mouths and pens of radicals. There is strong historical support for the radical position that the old nature-nurture polemic has a way of surfacing when those in power feel threatened by lower-class aspirations for social and economic mobility or when they feel the need to engage in some form of ruthless exploitation. Would 200 years of chattel slavery have been possible without the reassurance of those leaders, North and South, respected for their wisdom and righteousness, that the Negro was a different species, a different and lower order of humanity? It is a fact of American history that men with good academic credentials stepped forward at the turn of the century to apply Darwin's biological thesis to social situations and thereby provide the intellectual underpinnings for the brutal living and working conditions imposed on the immigrants of Southern and Eastern Europe who comprised the unskilled labor force. Historians are in substantial agreement that the naked oppression of nineteenth-century colonialism would have been difficult, if not impossible, without the concept of Anglo-Saxon-Teutonic natural superiority, a concept nourished by the late nineteenth-century press, pulpit, and university. The radicals now argue that Jensen, Herrnstein, and Eysenck are preparing the soil and climate for massive repression of those already ghettoized in the inner city. To the extent that these allegations are manifestations of paranoia or plain rhetorical hogwash (except for the name-calling involved), they do no real violence to anyone. But to the extent that these charges alert us to recognize and resist those who would trot out the shibboleth of genetic inadequacy as a "mask for privilege," to that extent the liberal is indebted to the radical.

The point also needs to be made that not once at any meeting I attended did I hear any talk, any suggestion, any proposal that would involve in any way violence, threats, or harassment of Dr. Herrnstein. In spite of statements to the contrary by students, faculty, the Harvard *Crimson*, the *Boston Globe*, and others, I can confirm as an eyewitness who attended every lecture that at no time in the semester was any lecture disrupted. As a matter of fact the SDS seemed to be unusually scrupulous about raising hands for recognition. I did notice, however, as the semester moved on, that Dr. Herrnstein became increasingly more selective about which raised hands he chose to select or acknowledge.

Most of these observations about the campus radical are made in retrospect. At the time I felt that on balance the SDS and UAG contributed more liabilities than assets to mounting support for a broad-based movement that would openly challenge Dr. Herrnstein.

Day by day my sense of indignation grew. Along with Herrnstein's course I was taking Burton White's course in the development of the preschool child, and I was becoming familiar with the literature that emphasizes the role of experience and environment in the development of intelligence. I was especially resentful of lectures and assignments that reiterated Jensen's generalization about the failure of compensatory education and was angered by the thought that all 300 of us were taught to accept as fact that very little can be done to raise IQ. It was particularly frustrating to hear a Herrnstein lecture in the morning and that same afternoon sit in Dr. White's class with a handful of graduate students and discuss the dramatic rise in IQ through early intervention that was being reported by Weikart, Heber, Smilansky, and other psychologists.

An incident occurred in class that convinced me that I must either act immediately or remain silent for the rest of the semester. A student and member of SDS raised his hand for recognition and complained to the class that Dr. Herrnstein made a statement to a black student after class to the effect that she was incapable of understanding certain points, a remark that the SDS student characterized as insulting and smacking of racism. Another SDS student raised the matter of the political implications of Herrnstein's article. At this point Dr. Brown halted further discussion and with class support, judging by the applause, set up ground rules that would limit class discussion to the subject of the nature of human intelligence.

That weekend I composed a letter, xeroxed 350 copies of it before class on the following Monday, arrived half an hour early, and distributed one each to my fellow students and professors:

To My Fellow Students in Social Science 15

October 12, 1971

I introduce myself to you as a classmate, a student at the Graduate School of Education, a high school teacher on leave of absence, and one who is unhappy about certain aspects of our course to date.

There is no question in my mind that the nature of human intelligence is an important and proper subject for study by psychologists, and I will accept the judgment of our instructors that this subject needs to take up more than 25 percent of the first semester of Harvard's only course in Introductory Psychology. But I have some doubts, uneasiness, "bad feelings" about the course that I feel the need to share with you.

It appears to me that the lectures to date and all of the assigned readings on the subject are designed to persuade, sell, manipulate the student into the belief that the

Jensen and Herrnstein thesis on the nature of human intelligence is the only hypothesis truly supported by the evidence. The Jensen and Herrnstein articles are the locus around which all discussion revolves, with critics of the thesis being required to refute, rebut, or otherwise assume a defensive position. Where are the lectures, literature, and studies that support the thesis that environment and the role of experience are of critical importance in the study of human intelligence? Where are the assigned readings that tell us about the Smilansky study (Jerusalem) and the Weikart study (Ypsilanti), both of which reported a rise of twenty points in IQ? Why no discussion on the significance of the Goldfarb study, which reported a 28 point difference in IQ between matched groups of children raised in foster homes and raised in institutions? Is it or is it not true that average IQ for American Indians on reservations is in the 80's but is over 100 for their brothers and sisters raised in white foster homes?

I admit to having mixed feelings about the ground rules for class discussion that Dr. Brown presented last week. On one hand I don't want our class interrupted with irrelevant discussion or personal exchanges, but on the other hand I don't think Dr. Herrnstein should disallow discussion on the *implications* of his thesis. I believe the author forfeited that right when he elected to publish his article in a popular magazine instead of a professional journal where his work could be scrutinized for accuracy and scholarship within the academic community by colleagues with credentials equal to his own. When a social scientist chooses to write for the nation, he has to assume some responsibility for the mischief that will occur when others use his thesis in the same way that the doctrine of Social Darwinism was used to inhibit the movement for reform and social change at the turn of the century. If 80 percent of "it" is there at birth, politicians will argue, why spend time, effort, and national treasure for improved environment and education of those "unfortunates" who just weren't born with "it."

I suppose I am especially frustrated at the thought of going back to my classroom to teach American history and being told by my white affluent students that a "Harvard professor" has "found out" that we white middle-class Americans are where *we are* and "they" are where *they are* not because of any violation of the democratic ideal and principle of equal opportunity and first-class citizenship for all, but simply because "nature so willed it."

If we really put our effort behind programs to provide the best possible environment for *every person* from conception through childhood, we could stop arguing over nature or nurture, genes or environment, and let the "intelligence chips" fall where they may.

If you think any of the points I make have merit, I hope some of you will join me in researching the literature on the role of experience in relation to human intelligence and making what we find available to our fellow students.

I also hope you will sign a letter with me urging the *Atlantic Monthly* to solicit an article from a psychologist that will give the other point of view.

Before and after the next class meeting a number of students sought me out to comment favorably on the letter. At least half a dozen asked for more information on the studies that I mentioned. It is difficult to judge what impact, if any, the letter had on the thinking of the students with regard to the subject of intelligence. A good number of the smiles and warm "good mornings" might have been born out of the titillation that people get when they see authority figures challenged.

Reaction from Dr. Herrnstein was to come via my "section head," Jeff Fine. I should explain that for our third session each week we were formed into small groups under the direction of a graduate or doctoral student, who reinforced the generalizations developed in the lectures and led us in class discussion. At our first meeting, prior to my writing the letter, I dominated class discussion with an attack on the case that the IQ test was a valid measure of human intelligence. After class Fine and I walked out together, and I accompanied him back to William James where we sat out front on one of the stone benches and talked. I tried to satisfy his curiosity about why I felt so strongly about the matter.

I explained that in my view Dr. Herrnstein had reached into every classroom of every public school in the country and without the hard evidence to justify this intrusion was doing violence to public education in three vital areas. To begin with he is erecting new barriers between psychological research and educational implementation of that research. Educators and the communities that support them are becoming aware that psychologists who specialize in human development are in substantial agreement that intellectual growth occurs in stages as the organism is stimulated by and interacts with his environment. The developing infant and toddler consumes his experiences, so to speak, and ingests them for growth to higher and higher levels of intellectual sophistication. Acceptance of this construct also implies acceptance of the idea that, as a proper diet is necessary for physical growth, so a balanced diet of experience is necessary for intellectual growth and that a child might look just fine physically yet be suffering from "intellectual malnutrition." Dr. Burton White believes that the period between eight and thirty months, when acquisition of language is taking place, is of particular importance. The thinking that guides the staff of the Brookline Early Education Project is that most developmental deficits of this kind in the very early years are not outgrown and when undetected and untreated have a way of multiplying, setting off chain reactions, causing new problems, some of which defy solution. This entire concept of human development sees the child bringing with him on his first day of formal schooling all the learning he has accumulated in his preschool experience. His capacity to cope successfully with the demands of school will be profoundly influenced by the preceding five years. The right amount of raw materials of experience will give one five year old the capital he needs to perform what has been identified as tasks and behavior appropriate for the age, while "missing parts" of early experience will put another child, of equal potential, under a severe handicap. At the very moment that thoughtful people are considering programs of early educational intervention, enter Richard Herrnstein wearing his Harvard credentials and waving his Stanford-Binet and telling the troubled taxpayer not to throw good money after bad genes.

The second point that I made to Jeff was that Dr. Herrnstein, again with insufficient evidence, would seriously disrupt the process of teaching and learning. We public school teachers know that whatever else is happening in the process, an essential ingredient in learning is *motivation*, which is largely a state of mind. The student must believe that he himself (not some genetic blueprint) is in control of what it takes to learn and achieve. What kind of public education can be built around teachers and children who have been persuaded by psychologists that intellectual inadequacy "may run in the genes of a family as certainly as bad teeth"?

Finally I told Jeff about my own syllogism, the one I developed while teaching black history to white middle-class students. It goes like this:

1. If people are largely the products of their environment and experience,
2. If white Americans imposed an environment and experience on black Americans designed to impoverish and humiliate,
3. If ideals such as fair play, equal opportunity, liberty, and justice equally available to all are in fact the philosophical underpinnings of our nation,
4. Then the present generation of white Americans must recognize their visceral as well as overt racism as a character defect and personality blemish and make a conscious effort to turn America around for the first time in the direction of its ideals and commitments.

Herrnstein's thesis, I argued, makes it perfectly possible to have high-sounding principles and ghettos at the same time.

Jeff listened to me attentively. The best that I could get out of him was an admission that some people might "misuse" the article, but he defended Dr. Herrnstein's motives. I don't know how much of my streetcorner lecture got back to Dr. Herrnstein, but the following week, a few days after the distribution of my letter, Jeff told me after class that Herrnstein wanted my references on Smilansky and Weikart; that he wanted to see the complete study. Another section head, with or without instructions, made it a point to confront me after class. He also asked for the references and then demanded to know why I did not ask to see Dr. Herrnstein if I had something on my mind and talk things over "man to man." I responded by saying that the time for "man to man" talk was before, not after, publication of his mischievous article. By this time I was so "psyched up" that I used these requests for references to make another attack in a three-page letter:

Another Point of View on
What IQ Tests Actually Measure

October 16, 1971

Dear Classmates,

Most of what we are studying is predicated on the belief that the IQ test is a valid measure of human intelligence. In spite of Dr. Brown's agreement not to use IQ and intelligence interchangeably, it is clear that the thesis presented makes no sense if this assumption is not made. I don't think anyone in class doubts that our instructors are satisfied that IQ is a reliable measure of human intelligence.

In 1963 Dr. Melvin M. Tumin, Professor of Sociology at Princeton, made a study of the work of Dr. Audrey Shuey, *The Testing of Negro Intelligence* (Lynchburg, Virginia, 1968). Dr. Shuey's study served as the basis for the thesis of Dr. Garrett and others that Negroes were innately less intelligent than whites, and it relied heavily, if not entirely, on IQ test scores.

Professor Tumin put questions regarding IQ to Dr. Henry C. Dyer who heads up ETS (Educational Testing Service) at Princeton. Dr. Dyer's credentials as one of the nation's foremost authorities on intelligence and ability testing are well known. He also put these questions to Dr. Silvan S. Tomkins, Professor of Psychology at Princeton, whose area of specialization is in the field of testing.

Since both men are considered authorities in the field of testing, I think their responses to the questions asked deserve your consideration when you decide to accept or reject the premise that IQ tests are a valid measure of human intelligence.

Question: Are there, in your judgment, any satisfactory tests of native, i.e., innate or inborn, intelligence? If you think there are, what are these tests? To what extent have the tests been able to free themselves of culturally specific factors, and thus become culture-free?

Dr. Dyer: There are no tests of native intelligence. In fact the concept of "native intelligence" is essentially meaningless. Every response to the stimulus material in intelligence tests is of necessity a *learned* response. The kind and amount of learning an individual acquires depends upon the experiences that come to him from the environment and upon his structural assets and liabilities. To some extent structural assets and liabilities are genetically determined; to some extent they are environmentally determined. With respect to many structural characteristics in an individual (visual acuity, for example), it is not possible to tell whether the characteristic in question has been genetically or environmentally determined. Therefore, there is no way of determining from an intelligence test score how much of the learning that produced it has been affected by genetic factors. So-called culture-free tests are built on one of two assumptions: (1) either the learning required to perform acceptably on the test is commonly and equally available to all people of all cultures, or (2) the stimulus material on the test is completely novel to all people of all cultures. Both assumptions are patently false.

Professor Tomkins: There are no completely satisfactory tests of native intelligence in my opinion, nor are there ways of getting reliable estimates of native intelligence other than those now in use.

Question: What do the standard intelligence tests test? Are we able, from the results of such tests, to make any valid inferences about native capacities? Under what conditions? Have these been observed in the volumes in front of you?

Dr. Dyer: (1) What do the standard intelligence tests test? They test how well an individual has learned to perform tasks like those on the test. Most such tasks are similar to those required of the student in school. Conse-

quently most of the standard intelligence tests test how
well the individual is likely to do in school. (2) Are we
able, from the results of such tests, to make any valid
inferences about native capacities? Obviously not. You
cannot make inferences about something that is meaningless.

Professor Tomkins: The standard intelligence tests test
achievements that permit an inference of intelligence to
the extent to which the following conditions have been
met: (1) all subjects have had the same motivation to
learn what is being tested; (2) all subjects are highly motivated to learn what is being tested; (3) all subjects have
had the same practice on what is being tested; (4) all
subjects have had sufficient practice so that the skill being
tested is overlearned so that extrapolation for insufficient
practice is not required and so that all can be compared
with respect to the same ceiling of ability; (5) all subjects
have had standardized guidance so that one can compare
performances independent of differential advantages,
and be sure that it is the same skill that is being tested;
(6) all subjects have been exposed to the same amount of
guidance as well as the same kind of guidance. It is for
these reasons that such a test as a vocabulary test so often
serves as an excellent test of intelligence. To the extent,
however, to which some individuals are less motivated to
communicate verbally, to the extent to which such motivation is not very high in all subjects, to the extent to
which all subjects have not had the same amount of practice, the same exposure to standardized guidance, and to
the same amount of guidance, direct and indirect,
through exposure to models who speak and use language
more or less expertly, this test fails as a general test of
intelligence. There are at present no tests that meet entirely all the criteria that are necessary to assess correctly
the innate potential. In varying degrees they all reflect
the impact of differences in motivation, practice, and
guidance as these occur in different societies.

I hope you will sign the letter to the *Atlantic Monthly.*

I was pleased to note that this time Dr. Herrnstein
came out of the lecture hall into the corridor to request
a copy from me. He made no comment as the class came
to order, nor did he refer to the letter in his next lecture.
This lack of response created some support and sympa-

thy for me among students who wanted no part of an SDS
polemic but felt that the content of both letters called for
something more than silence.

I suspect that the letter circulated among the faculty at
William James because some weeks later at a public meeting, Dr. Newman, current chairman of the Psychology
Department, alluded to it and remarked sarcastically that
if I thought that Dr. Dyer and Dr. Herrnstein disagreed
on IQ testing, then "I did not read very well."

The petition I referred to which I was circulating at this
time was a letter to the *Atlantic Monthly* describing the
irresponsible use to which an article of this kind would be
put and requesting the editors to help undo the mischief
for which they were partly responsible by commissioning
an article from another psychologist who would make the
case for the role of experience and environment in intellectual development.

It was difficult to get the petition to all of the students.
Most of them would pile into class at 10:00 A.M. or a few
minutes after and dash off as soon as class was over. I had
no choice but to circulate the petition during class, and
at times it would get stalled or go back in the direction
from which it had just come. I know it never reached all
of the students, and so I was not too unhappy with the
more than one hundred signatures I had by the end of the
week. It was painful, however, to see a member of a
minority group read or scan it and pass it along unsigned.
I saw this happen in the case of a couple of black students
and a good many of the Oriental students.

It developed later that one of the section heads signed
the petition, and when the editors furnished him with a
copy of the signed petition Dr. Herrnstein severely
rebuked this person. The SDS tried to make a big thing
of the reprimand. Herrnstein came out of it rather well
by admitting that he had lost his temper and that he
might be something of a "curmudgeon" and, of course,
keeping the section head as a member of his staff.

GETTING NOWHERE FAST

Prior to mailing the petition I tried to get some faculty signatures. Harvard's Graduate School of Education, I reasoned, would be the best place to go. After all, in the final analysis what is education if it is not identifying and providing the environment and experiences that will nourish human development? Humanistic considerations aside, as a matter of self-interest, anyone in education, the whole spectrum from the deeply dedicated to those who are just making a living, is threatened by Jensen and Herrnstein and should be the first to support efforts to drag these psychologists to the academic witness stand for searing cross-examination.

I mailed, first class, a copy of my petition to every member of the faculty of the School of Education, administrators included. I am serious when I confess that I skipped class two days later, stayed home, and waited for the mailman. I was actually concerned that the stack of responses would be too much for my little mailbox and the mailman might return the whole pile to the post office. Out of more than 100 letters mailed, I received two signatures: one from an office secretary and one from a dean who also holds political office in Cambridge. I also received a letter from psychologist David McClelland. He enclosed a draft of a paper he was writing that deplores the promiscuous use of all kinds of testing by psychologists, but he declined to sign the petition because he felt that it was an attack on the spirit of free inquiry.

My petition went off, registered mail, without faculty signatures. About a week later I received a cryptic letter from Mr. Manning, editor of the *Atlantic*, thanking me for my letter, thoroughly disagreeing with the points made, and informing me that the *Atlantic* considers manuscripts for publication on the basis of merit.

In the meantime the SDS and UAG pressed on with attacks on Professor Herrnstein. They handed out leaflets, held rallies, had demonstrations, and confronted administrators on every level with demands for Herrnstein's dismissal. This pressure, together perhaps with my letter writing activity, made it impossible for Dr. Herrnstein to avoid an open discussion. A special class was scheduled at which time Herrnstein agreed to answer all questions on all aspects and implications of his article. Although attendance was optional for our class, at the appointed time every seat in the lecture hall was filled, about one-third Soc. Sci. 15 students and the rest strange faces, many, I suspect, from off campus. The meeting was opened by Dr. Brown, who defended the course content by calling attention to one assigned article by Stichecombe on the role of environment, the fact that J. McVicker Hunt's book *Intelligence and Experience* is listed on the bibliography of "Further Readings," and denied that he had any commitment to present both sides of all issues. I made a statement, criticizing the course content and challenging Dr. Brown to either present both sides or reveal his bias. I made the mistake of limiting my comments to criticism of the course content, which took me into psychology, a field in which I am weak. I would have done better to concentrate on the implication of the article for public education, a field in which I am stronger. There was a certain amount of heckling, which bothered me and broke my train of thought. Members of the SDS and UAG peppered Herrnstein with questions and comments, most of which carried the charge of racism and suggested his involvement in "the conspiracy." Herrnstein managed a look of long suffering as a response to charges of dark and dire racist motives and played to the full the role of the honest and intrepid scholar who has offered himself up to the slings and arrows of these irresponsible radicals in his quest for truth. He came out of it rather well, I thought.

The open meeting took the steam out of the anti-Herrnstein activity. I continued to write letters, presenting data that I maintained revealed the assumption of Dr. Jensen about the failure of compensatory education to be unscholarly. These letters and the leaflets handed out by the SDS went largely ignored. By this time we were on a new unit, and most of the class felt that the termination of the unit on intelligence ought also to mark the end of the polemic. We had a midterm exam, the kind that is taken home and prepared more like a term paper. I bristled when I saw question 4, which asked us (with no limitation on time or money) to outline what we would do to find out the reason why the mean IQ score of white Americans might be ten points higher than the score of a recently discovered primitive tribe in the Philippines on a culture-fair test. I had a good time composing a satirical response. I first raised the point that I would have to check the test against Dr. Dyer's requirements for a culture-fair test: that either the learning required to perform acceptably was commonly and equally available to both Filipinos and Americans or that the stimulus material on the test was completely novel to both cultures. Then I suggested studying the childrearing practices. If no explanation of the ten-point diffference came out of this study, I would then recruit men and women of childbearing age from each culture, administer IQ tests, and grade them (H) for high, (A) for average, and (L) for low. I would then pair off the couples, administer a fertility drug, and have them engage in that biological performance common to both cultures, so that I would have samples of twins, triplets, quadruplets, etc., in combinations of inherited IQ of HH, HA, HL, AA, AL, and LL. I would separate them at birth into contrived environments, enriched (EE), average (EA), and deprived (ED). Enriched is defined as an environment that includes everything that scientists and social scientists can tell us about optimum conditions for human development. Subjects in EE would be told over and over again from the earliest age, that they were born into the top social class, derive from highly intelligent and highly respected parents, and have already been accepted by Harvard. I defined a deprived environment (ED) as one in which there is a minimum of physical care, stimulus, maternal interaction, and verbal interaction plus exposure to those conditions normally associated with poverty. Subjects in ED would be made aware over and over again, from the earliest age, that they occupy the lowest class in society, derive from low-class parents, that their parents were not too bright and that they are not too bright.

Some of the subjects would be kept in constant environments; others would be switched at various points during development. At the appropriate time we would administer the "culture-fair" IQ test to all of the subjects and see what kind of correlations existed for identical progeny raised in various environments and how scores correlated with scores of the natural parents. It would be especially interesting to note how an HH subject made out in an ED environment and how an LL subject developed in an EE environment. I observed that my study would give us good evidence to settle, once and for all, the nature-nurture polemic. I concluded by saying that those psychologists who might be offended by the study and object to it on ethical grounds ought to direct some objection and indignation to colleagues who make professional judgments on genetic endowments for intelligence based on a single IQ test, without a serious attempt to define the variables "environment" and "experience."

My paper was returned with a grade of "excellent." I am reasonably sure that the section head who read it did not bring it to the attention of Dr. Herrnstein. Satirical midterms were one thing and effective challenge to Dr. Herrnstein was quite another.

CRIMSON ADVERTISEMENTS

I was still reading the literature on the effect of early educational intervention on IQ and subsequent school performance. My association with the Brookline Early Education program gave me access to data that made me confident that assumptions about the inefficacy of compensatory education would soon be widely challenged. I also consoled myself with the thought that most social scientists probably disagreed with Herrnstein, privately deplored the article, and were critical of the property of publishing articles of this sort in popular magazines rather than in professional journals. I was, therefore, totally unprepared for the headline in the Harvard *Crimson* that greeted me the morning of November 24: "Herrnstein Obtains Faculty Support." The story stated that 107 members of the Harvard faculty had contributed to an advertisement condemning "personal attacks" on Richard Herrnstein. The following Monday a similar advertisement appeared in the *Crimson* over the signature of 107 members of the faculty.

The word "harassment" appeared in the copy three times. The story in the *Crimson* of the previous Wednesday reported that the statement had been drafted by Archibald Cox, a Williston Professor of Law. If Professor Cox selected the word "harassment," he surely intended to convey the impression that Dr. Herrnstein was "harassed" in the sense that lawyers and law enforcement officers use the term.

I assumed that the statement was accurate and telephoned Hilary Putnam to tell him what I thought of him and his cronies for their Mafia-like tactics. Dr. Putnam absolutely denied that he or any member of his group had done anything that could possibly be construed as harassment. Later that week students and tutors at Dunster

House raised questions in the Harvard *Crimson* on the details of the harassment that Dr. Herrnstein and his family had suffered. It turned out that the word was used to describe false, slanderous, and inaccurate statements made by the SDS about Dr. Herrnstein.

I am still amazed that 107 distinguished members of the faculty would find it unreasonable that an article so laden with political implications would produce a political response, and I am still disappointed that "scholars" would put their name to such a statement, without verifying the accuracy of the charge "harassment."

Apart from the statement of harassment, I was stunned by other aspects of the text. There was not much doubt that people in high academic posts and leaders of intellectual thought considered Social Darwinism to be legitimate scholarship. Instead of sleeping that night, I composed a message of my own and the following morning took it to the *Crimson* office on Plympton Street and ordered it run as an advertisement, equal in size to that run by the 107 faculty members.

A Letter to Harvard's Faculty Concerning the Herrnstein Matter

As a student of Dr. Herrnstein, a public school teacher on leave of absence, and an individual with no radical connections, on or off campus, I would like to give you the reasons why I feel the Harvard faculty should make some public statement expressing disapproval of Dr. Herrnstein and his article in the *Atlantic Monthly*.

What is involved here is that one of your colleagues, with no special credentials in psychometrics, genetics, sociology, economics, or philosophy, and for reasons best known to himself, did all of the following things:

•He took extraordinary liberties as to inferences which can properly be drawn from IQ test scores.

•He ignored published data which reveals that high scores on tests for creativity and high scores for IQ do not correlate, a fact which is relevant to the subject under discussion.

•He selected those twin studies which support his view

but made no mention of other twin studies dissonant to his view.

•He adopted Dr. Jensen's unscholarly assumption about the failure of compensatory education.

•He failed to employ that caution and diffidence usually assumed by scientists and social scientists who study the relationship between genetic endowment for intelligence and that complex variable of experience and environment with which it is inextricably bound.

•With no fresh data and on the basis of the "evidence and scholarship" indicated above, he wrote a pseudo-scientific article for a popular magazine in which he made sweeping generalizations about the predetermined intellectual equipment of our nation's lower socioeconomic groups and concluded that their place on the bottom of the social and economic pyramid was inevitable.

•He then cooperated in the publication of countless "summaries" in news magazines and newspapers throughout the country inviting any mischief-maker, segregationist, foe of public education, force for reaction, in public office or out, to use in his own way and for his own purposes "the findings of the chairman of the Department of Psychology at Harvard University."

•Finally, at a time in our nation's history when we white Americans (some of us kicking and screaming) are being brought into a wholesome confrontation with the contradictions and immorality of our overt and visceral racism, Dr. Herrnstein offers a "way out" of what Gunnar Myrdal has called "The American Dilemma" and casts a cloak of respectability over a new version of Social Darwinism.

Call it what you will, this is not legitimate scholarship! There are many of us, on and off campus, who look to the Harvard faculty for *humanistic* as well as intellectual leadership. For this reason and for ethical considerations involved, Dr. Herrnstein should be censured, repudiated, or otherwise rebuked by his colleagues.

"To sin by silence when they should protest, makes cowards of men." (A. Lincoln)

Following both advertisements, a flurry of letters appeared in the *Crimson* and the *Boston Globe* on both sides of the issue. The *Crimson* ran an editorial critical of Herrnstein, together with another editorial in support of Herrnstein. The December issue of the *Atlantic* printed a number of pages of letters "for and against," with a final response by Herrnstein as "the last word."

The morning that my advertisement appeared, I received a telephone call from Nobel Prize winner George Wald, complimenting me on its substance. This was to be the last kind word I was to receive from the liberal academic community. I sent copies of my advertisement to a number of well-known people in the social sciences, asking that they lend their name and prestige to the proposition that the Herrnstein article was not within the parameters of legitimate scholarship.

I still find the responses painful when I reread them. In general they were critical of me for running the advertisement and especially for asking the faculty to repudiate, rebuke, or censure Dr. Herrnstein. The general thrust of the criticism falls into two categories: the first is a Voltaire-like statement about disagreeing with what Herrnstein says but defending his right to say it, and the second describes me as a self-styled censor who would shut off free inquiry because I believe society is better left in "ignorance."

It is difficult to respond to these charges in the abstract. For purposes of clarification I offer consideration of the hypothesis that:

Tendency toward patterns of behavior is chemically encoded in the genes, with certain behavior characteristic of ethnic and racial groups being a consequence of the genetic pool of the group.

Would the 107 Harvard faculty repeat the same statement with regard to this hypothesis as they made in support of Dr. Herrnstein?

The soundness of his argument, and the reliability of the underlying data and any *implications for public policy* are all appropriate subjects for debate and continuous reexamination in the light of new knowledge and experience. [My italics]

Would underlying data in the form of statistics about felonious assaults with razors by Negroes, Italians in organized crime, and fraudulent insurance claims by Jews be "appropriate subjects for debate"? What about these implications for public policy? Perhaps license sale of weapons to Negroes, maintain special surveillance of Italians, and permit insurance companies to raise rates for Jews as they do for teen-age male drivers.

The basis for the analogy comes from the fact that to be labeled "unintelligent" in our culture not only handicaps a person in the contest for the better things in life but also makes it virtually impossible to develop any sense of self-respect or a wholesome self-image. All the synonyms for the word "unintelligent," including the old as well as the new slang, carry a derisive connotation. People so identified are common targets for ridicule and contempt.

I do not question that human intelligence is a proper subject for scientific research. I argue only that those who undertake such research be bound by a code of conduct that requires that *the amount of "hard" evidence in support of the hypothesis be in direct relation to the social and political implications of that hypothesis.* A psychologist enjoys no special dispensation to shoot off hypotheses and disclaim responsibility for the pain and damage done to those wounded by these psychological "shots."

I submit that by its silence the academic community has encouraged the Jensens, Herrnsteins, and Eysencks to revive what is essentially a doctrine of Social Darwinism and deliver it through a cooperative and eager press to a public desperately seeking to avoid the bitter cup of racial equality. This community needs to redefine its parameters of legitimate scholarship or be judged harshly by those of us who deal with the damage done by the mischief makers.

Testing for Competence Rather Than for "Intelligence"*

DAVID C. McCLELLAND

The testing movement in the United States has been a success, if one judges success by the usual American criteria of size, influence, and profitability. Intelligence and aptitude tests are used nearly everywhere by schools, colleges, and employers. It is a sign of backwardness not to have test scores in the school records of children. The Educational Testing Service alone employs about 2,000 people, annually administers Scholastic Aptitude Tests to thousands of aspirants to college, and makes enough money to support a large basic research operation. Its tests have tremendous power over the lives of young people by stamping some of them "qualified" and others "less qualified" for college work. Until recent "exceptions" were made (over the protest of some), the tests have served as a very efficient device for screening out black, Spanish-speaking, and other minority applicants to colleges. Admissions officers have protested that they

SOURCE: David C. McClelland, "Testing for Competence Rather than for 'Intelligence,' " *American Psychologist* 28 (1973): 1–14. Copyright 1973 by the American Psychological Association. Reprinted by permission.

*This article contains the substance of remarks made at a public lecture given at the Educational Testing Service, Princeton, New Jersey, January 4, 1971.

take other qualities besides test achievements into account in granting admission, but careful studies by Wing and Wallach (1971) and others have shown that this is true only to a very limited degree.

Why should intelligence or aptitude tests have all this power? What justifies the use of such tests in selecting applicants for college entrance or jobs? On what assumptions is the success of the movement based? They deserve careful examination before we go on rather blindly promoting the use of tests as instruments of power over the lives of many Americans.

The key issue is obviously the *validity* of so-called intelligence tests. Their use could not be justified unless they were valid, and it is my conviction that the evidence for their validity is by no means so overwhelming as most of us, rather unthinkingly, had come to think it was. In point of fact, most of us just believed the results that the testers gave us, without subjecting them to the kind of fierce skepticism that greets, for example, the latest attempt to show that ESP exists. My objectives are to review skeptically the main lines of evidence for the validity of intelligence and aptitude tests and to draw some inferences from this review as to new lines that testing might take in the future.

Let us grant at the outset that brain-damaged or retarded people do less well on intelligence tests than other people. Wechsler (1958) initially used this criterion to validate his instrument, although it has an obvious weakness: brain-damaged people do less well on almost *any* test so that it is hard to argue that something unique called "lack of intelligence" is responsible for the deficiency in test scores. The multimethod, multitrait criterion has not been applied here.

TESTS PREDICT GRADES IN SCHOOL

The games people are required to play on aptitude tests are similar to the games teachers require in the classroom. In fact, many of Binet's original tests were taken from exercises that teachers used in French schools. So it is scarcely surprising that aptitude test scores are correlated highly with grades in school. The whole Scholastic Aptitude Testing movement rests its case largely on this single undeniable fact. Defenders of intelligence testing, like McNemar (1964), often seem to be suggesting that this is the only kind of validity necessary. McNemar remarked that "the manual of the Differential Aptitude Test of the Psychological Corporation contains a staggering total of 4,096, yes I counted 'em, validity coefficients." What more could you ask for, ladies and gentlemen? It was not until I looked at the manual myself (McNemar certainly did not enlighten me) that I confirmed my suspicion that almost every one of those "validity" coefficients involved predicting grades in courses—in other words, performing on similar types of tests.

So what about grades? How valid are they as predictors? Researchers have in fact had great difficulty demonstrating that grades in school are related to any other behaviors of importance—other than doing well on aptitude tests. Yet the general public—including many psychologists and most college officials—simply has been unable to believe or accept this fact. It seems so self-evident to educators that those who do well in their classes *must* go on to do better in life that they systematically have disregarded evidence to the contrary that has been accumulating for some time. In the early 1950s, a committee of the Social Science Research Council of which I was chairman looked into the matter and concluded that while grade level attained seemed related to future measures of success in life, performance within grade was related only slightly. In other words, being a high school or college graduate gave one a credential that opened up certain higher level jobs, but the poorer students in high school or college did as well in life as the top students. As a college teacher, I found this hard to believe until I made a simple check. I took the top eight students in a class in the late 1940s at Wesleyan University where I was teaching—all straight A students—and contrasted what they were doing in the early 1960s with what eight really poor students were doing—all of whom were getting barely passing averages in college (C— or below). To my great surprise, I could not distinguish the two lists of men fifteen to eighteen years later. There were lawyers, doctors, research scientists, and college and high school teachers in both groups. The only difference I noted was that those with better grades got into better law or medical schools, but even with this supposed advantage they did not have notably more successful careers as compared with the poorer students who had had to be satisfied with "second-rate" law and medical schools at the outset. Doubtless the C— students could not get into even second-rate law and medical schools under the stricter admissions testing standards of today. Is that an advantage for society?

Such outcomes have been documented carefully by many researchers (cf. Hoyt, 1965) both in Britain (Hudson, 1960) and in the United States. Berg (1970), in a book suggestively titled *Education and Jobs: The Great Training Robbery*, has summarized studies showing that neither amount of education nor grades in school are related to vocational success as a factory worker, bank teller, or air traffic controller. Even for highly intellectual jobs like scientific researcher, Taylor, Smith, and Ghiselin (1963) have shown that superior on-the-job performance is related in no way to better grades in college. The average college grade for the top third in research success was 2.73 (about B—), and for the bottom third, 2.69 (also B—). Such facts have been known for some time. They make it abundantly clear that the testing movement is in grave danger of perpetuating a mythological meritocracy in which none of the measures of merit bears significant demonstrable validity with respect to any measures outside of the charmed circle. Psychologists used to say as a kind of an "in" joke that intelligence is what the intelligence tests measure. That seems to be uncomfortably near the whole truth and nothing but the truth. But what's funny about it, when the public took us more seriously than we did ourselves and used the tests to screen people out of opportunities for education and high-status jobs? And why call excellence at these test games intelligence?

Even further, why keep the best education for those who are already doing well at the games? This in effect is what the colleges are doing when they select from their applicants those with the highest Scholastic Aptitude Test scores. Isn't this like saying that we will coach especially those who already can play tennis well? One would think that the purpose of education is precisely to improve the performance of those who are not doing very well. So when psychologists predict on the basis of the Scholastic Aptitude Test who is most likely to do well in college, they are suggesting implicitly that these are the "best bets" to admit. But in another sense, if the colleges were interested in proving that they could educate people, high-scoring students might be poor bets because they would be less likely to show improvement in performance. To be sure, the teachers want students who will do well in their courses, but should society allow the teachers to determine who deserves to be educated, particularly when the performance of interest to teachers bears so little relation to any other type of life performance?

DO INTELLIGENCE TESTS TAP ABILITIES THAT ARE RESPONSIBLE FOR JOB SUCCESS?

Most psychologists think so; certainly the general public thinks so (Cronbach, 1970, p. 300), but the evidence is a whole lot less satisfactory than one would think it ought to be to justify such confidence.

Thorndike and Hagen (1959), for instance, obtained 12,000 correlations between aptitude test scores and various measures of later occupational success on over 10,000 respondents and concluded that the number of significant correlations did not exceed what would be expected by chance. In other words, the tests were invalid. Yet psychologists go on using them, trusting that the poor validities must be due to restriction in range due to the fact that occupations do not admit individuals with lower scores. But even here it is not clear whether the characteristics required for entry are, in fact, essential to success in the field. One might suppose that finger dexterity is essential to being a dentist, and require a minimum test score for entry. Yet, it was found by Thorndike and Hagen (1959) to be related negatively to income as a dentist! Holland and Richards (1965) and Elton and Shevel (1969) have shown that no consistent relationships exist between scholastic aptitude scores in college students and their *actual accomplishments* in social leadership, the arts, science, music, writing, and speech and drama.

Yet what are we to make of Ghiselli's (1966, p. 121) conclusions, based on a review of 50 years of research, that general intelligence tests correlate .42 with trainability and .23 with proficiency across all types of jobs? Each of these correlations is based on over 10,000 cases. It is small wonder that psychologists believe intelligence tests are valid predictors of job success. Unfortunately, it is impossible to evaluate Ghiselli's conclusion, as he does not cite his sources, and he does not state exactly how job proficiency was measured for each of his correlations. We can draw some conclusions from his results, however, and we can make a good guess that job proficiency often was measured by supervisors' ratings or by such indirect indicators of supervisors' opinions as turnover, promotion, salary increases, and the like.

What is interesting to observe is that intelligence test correlations with proficiency in higher status jobs are regularly higher than with proficiency in lower status jobs (Ghiselli, 1966, pp. 34, 78). Consider the fact that intelligence test scores correlate $-.08$ with proficiency as a canvasser or solicitor and $.45$ with proficiency as a stock and bond salesman. This should be a strong clue as to what intelligence tests are getting at, but most observers have overlooked it or simply assumed that it takes more general ability to be a stock and bond salesman than a canvasser. But these two jobs differ also in social status, in the language, accent, clothing, manner, and connections by education and family necessary for success in the job. The basic problem with many job proficiency measures for validating ability tests is that they depend heavily on the *credentials* the man brings to the job—the habits, values, accent, interests, etc.—that mean he is acceptable to management and to clients. Since we also know that social class background is related to getting higher ability test scores (Nuttall & Fozard, 1970), as well as to having the right personal credentials for success, *the correlation between intelligence test scores and job success often may be an artifact,* the product of their joint association with class status. Employers may have a right to select bond salesmen who have gone to the right schools because they do better, but psychologists do not have a right to argue that it is their *intelligence* that makes them more proficient in their jobs.

We know that correlation does not equal causation, but we keep forgetting it. Far too many psychologists still

report average-ability test scores for high- and low-pre-
stige occupations, inferring incorrectly that this evidence
shows it takes more of this type of brains to perform a
high-level than a low-level job. For instance, Jensen
(1972) wrote recently:

Can the I.Q. tell us anything of practical importance? Is
it related to our commonsense notions about mental ability as we ordinarily think of it in connection with educational and occupational performance? Yes, indeed, and
there is no doubt about it. . . . The I.Q. obtained after 9
or 10 years of age also predicts final adult occupational
status to almost as high a degree as it predicts scholastic
performance. . . . The *average* I.Q. of persons within a
particular occupation is closely related to that occupation's standing in terms of average income and the
amount of prestige accorded to it by the general public.

He certainly leaves the impression that it is "mental ability as we ordinarily think of it" that is responsible for this
association between average IQ scores and job prestige.
But the association can be interpreted as meaning, just as
reasonably, that it takes more *pull,* more opportunity, to
get the vocabulary and other habits required by those in
power from incumbents of high-status positions. Careful
studies that try to separate the *credential* factor from the
ability factor in job success have been very few in number.

Ghiselli (1966) simply did not deal with the problem of
what the criteria of job proficiency may mean for validating the tests. For example, he reported a correlation of
.27 between intelligence test scores and proficiency as a
policeman or a detective (p. 83), with no attention given
to the very important issues involved in how a policeman's performance is to be evaluated. Will supervisors'
ratings do? If so, it discriminates against black policemen
(Baehr, Furcon, and Froemel, 1968) because white supervisors regard them as inferior. And what about the public? Shouldn't its opinion as to how they are served by the
police be part of the criterion? The most recent careful
review (Kent and Eisenberg, 1972) of the evidence relat-

ing ability test scores to police performance concluded that there is no stable, significant relationship. Here is concrete evidence that one must view with considerable skepticism the assumed relation of intelligence test scores to success on the job.

One other illustration may serve to warn the unwary about accepting uncritically simple statements about the role of ability, as measured by intelligence tests, in life outcomes. It is stated widely that intelligence promotes general adjustment and results in lower neuroticism. For example, Anderson (1960) reported a significant correlation between intelligence test scores obtained from boys in 1950, age fourteen to seventeen, and follow-up ratings of general adjustment made five years later. Can we assume that intelligence promotes better adjustment to life as has been often claimed? It sounds reasonable until we reflect that the "intelligence" test is a test of ability to do well in school (to take academic-type tests), that many of Anderson's sample were still in school or getting started on careers, and that those who are not doing well in school or getting a good first job because of it are likely to be considered poorly adjusted by themselves and others. Here the test has become part of the criterion and has introduced the correlation artificially. In case this sounds like special reasoning, consider the fact, not commented on particularly by Anderson, that the same correlation between "intelligence" test scores and adjustment in girls was an insignificant .06. Are we to conclude that intelligence does *not* promote adjustment in girls? It would seem more reasonable to argue that the particular ability tested, here associated with scholastic success, is more important to success (and hence adjustment) for boys than for girls. But this is a far cry from the careless inference that intelligence tests tap a general ability to adapt successfully to life's problems because high-IQ children (read "men") have better mental health (Jensen, 1972).

To make the point even more vividly, suppose you are

a ghetto resident in the Roxbury section of Boston. To qualify for being a policeman you have to take a three-hour-long general intelligence test in which you must know the meaning of words like "quell," "pyromaniac," and "lexicon." If you do not know enough of those words or cannot play analogy games with them, you do not qualify and must be satisfied with some such job as being a janitor for which an "intelligence" test is not required yet by the Massachusetts Civil Service Commission. You, not unreasonably, feel angry, upset, and unsuccessful. Because you do not know those words, you are considered to have low intelligence, and since you consequently have to take a low-status job and are unhappy, you contribute to the celebrated correlations of low intelligence with low occupational status and poor adjustment. Psychologists should be ashamed of themselves for promoting a view of general intelligence that has encouraged such a testing program, particularly when there is no solid evidence that significantly relates performance on this type of intelligence test with performance as a policeman.

THE ROLE OF POWER IN CONTROLLING LIFE-OUTCOME CRITERIA

Psychologists have been, until recently, incredibly naïve about the role of powerful interests in controlling the criteria against which psychologists have validated their tests. Terman felt that his studies had proved conclusively that "giftedness," as he measured it with psychological tests, was a key factor in life success. By and large, psychologists have agreed with him. Kohlberg, LaCrosse, and Ricks (1970), for instance, in a recent summary statement concluded that Terman and Oden's (1947) study "indicated the gifted were more successful occupationally, maritally, and socially than the average group, and were lower in 'morally deviant' forms of psychopathology (e.g., alcoholism, homosexuality)." Jensen (1972) agreed:

One of the most convincing demonstrations that I.Q. is related to "real life" indicators of ability was provided in a classic study by Terman and his associates at Stanford University. . . . Terman found that for the most part these high-I.Q. children in later adulthood markedly excelled the general population on every indicator of achievement that was examined: a higher level of education completed; more scholastic honors and awards; higher occupational status; higher income; production of more articles, books, patents and other signs of creativity; more entries in *Who's Who;* a lower mortality rate; better physical and mental health; and a lower divorce rate. . . . Findings such as these establish beyond a doubt that I.Q. tests measure characteristics that are obviously of considerable importance in our present technological society. To say that the kind of ability measured by intelligence tests is irrelevant or unimportant would be tantamount to repudiating civilization as we know it.

I do not want to repudiate civilization as we know it, or even to dismiss intelligence tests as irrelevant or unimportant, but I do want to state, as emphatically as possible, that Terman's studies do *not* demonstrate unequivocally that it is the kind of ability measured by the intelligence tests that is responsible for (i.e., causes) the greater success of the high-IQ children. Terman's studies *may* show only that the rich and powerful have more opportunities, and therefore do better in life. And if that is even possibly true, it is socially irresponsible to state that psychologists have established "beyond a doubt" that the kind of ability measured by intelligence tests is essential for high-level performance in our society. For, by current methodological standards, Terman's studies (and others like them) were naïve. No attempt was made to equate for *opportunity* to be successful occupationally and socially. His gifted people clearly came from superior socioeconomic backgrounds to those he compared them

TABLE 1 **Numbers of Students in Various IQ and SES Categories (Sixth Grade) and Percentage Subsequently Going to College**

IQ	Socioeconomic Status			
	High	Percentage to College	Low	Percentage to College
High	51	71	57	23
Low	33	18	96	5

Note. $\chi^2 = 11.99$, $p < .01$, estimated tetrachoric $\tau = .35$, SES × IQ. (Table adapted from Havighurst et al., 1962. Copyrighted by Wiley, 1962.)

with (at one point all men in California, including day laborers). He had no unequivocal evidence that it was "giftedness" (as reflected in his test scores) that was responsible for the superior performance of his group. It would be *as* legitimate (though also not proven) to conclude that sons of the rich, powerful, and educated were apt to be more successful occupationally, maritally, and socially because they had more material advantages. To make the point in another way, consider the data in Table 1, which are fairly representative of findings in this area. They were obtained by Havighurst, Bowman, Liddle, Matthews, and Pierce (1962) from a typical town in Middle America. One observes the usual strong relationship between social class and IQ and between IQ and college-going—which leads on to occupational success. The traditional interpretation of such findings is that more stupid children come from the lower classes because their parents are also stupid which explains why they are lower class. A higher proportion of children with high IQ go to college because they are more intelligent and more suited to college study. This is as it should be because IQ predicts academic success. The fact that more intelligent people going to college come more often from the upper class follows naturally because the upper classes contain more intelligent people. So the traditional argument has gone for years. It seemed all very simple and obvious to Terman and his followers.

However, a closer look at Table 1 suggests another interpretation that is equally plausible, though not more required by the data than the one just given. Compare the percentages going to college in the "deviant" boxes— high socioeconomic status and low IQ versus high IQ and low socioeconomic status. It appears to be no more likely for the bright children (high IQ) from the lower classes to go to college (despite their high aptitude for it) than for the "stupid" children from the upper classes. Why is this? An obvious possibility is that the bright but poor children do not have the money to go to college, or they do not want to go, preferring to work or do other things. In the current lingo, they are "disadvantaged" in the sense that they have not had access to the other factors (values, aspirations, money) that promote college-going in upper-class children. But now we have an alternative explanation of college-going—namely, socioeconomic status which seems to be as good a predictor of this type of success as ability. How can we claim that ability as measured by these tests is the critical factor in college-going? Very few children, even with good test-taking ability, go to college if they are from poor families. One could argue that they are victims of oppression: they do not have the opportunity or the values that permit or encourage going to college. Isn't it likely that the same oppressive forces may have prevented even more of them from learning to play school games well at all?

Belonging to the power elite (high socioeconomic status) not only helps a young man go to college and get jobs through contacts his family has, it also gives him easy access as a child to the credentials that permit him to get into certain occupations. Nowadays, those credentials include the words and word-game skills used in Scholastic Aptitude Tests. In the Middle Ages they required knowledge of Latin for the learned professions of law, medicine, and theology. Only those young men who could read and write Latin could get into those occupations, and if tests had been given in Latin, I am sure they would have shown that professionals scored higher in Latin than men in general, that sons who grew up in families where Latin was used would have an advantage in those tests compared to those in poor families where Latin was unknown, and that these men were more likely to get into the professions. But would we conclude we were dealing with a general ability factor? Many a ghetto resident must or should feel that he is in a similar position with regard to the kind of English he must learn in order to do well on tests, in school, and in occupations today in America. I was recently in Jamaica where all around me poor people were speaking an English that was almost entirely incomprehensible to me. If I insisted, they would speak patiently in a way that I could understand, but I felt like a slow-witted child. I have wondered how well I would do in Jamaican society if this kind of English were standard among the rich and powerful (which, by the way, it is not), and therefore required by them for admission into their better schools and occupations (as determined by a test administered perhaps by the Jamaican Testing Service). I would feel oppressed, not less intelligent, as the test would doubtless decide I was because I was so slow of comprehension and so ignorant of ordinary vocabulary.

When Cronbach (1970) concluded that such a test "is giving realistic information on the presence of a handicap," he is, of course, correct. But psychologists should recognize that it is those in power in a society who often decide what is a handicap. We should be a lot more cautious about accepting as ultimate criteria of ability the standards imposed by whatever group happens to be in power.

Does this mean that intelligence tests are invalid? As so often when you examine a question carefully in psychology, the answer depends on what you mean. Valid for what? Certainly they are valid for predicting who will get ahead in a number of prestige jobs where credentials are important. So is white skin: it too is a valid predictor of job success in prestige jobs. But no one would argue that white skin per se is an ability factor. Lots of the celebrated correlations between so-called intelligence test scores and success can lay no greater claim to representing an ability factor.

Valid for predicting success in school? Certainly, because school success depends on taking similar types of tests. Yet, neither the tests nor school grades seem to have much power to predict real competence in many life outcomes, aside from the advantages that credentials convey on the individuals concerned.

Are there *no* studies which show that general intelligence test scores predict competence with all of these other factors controlled? I can only assert that I have had a very hard time finding a good carefully controlled study of the problem because testers simply have not worked very hard on it: they have believed so much that they were measuring true competence that they have not bothered to try to prove that they were. Studies do exist, of course, which show significant positive correlations between special test scores and job-related skills. For example, perceptual speed scores are related to clerical proficiency. So are tests of vocabulary, immediate memory, substitution, and arithmetic. Motor ability test scores are related to proficiency as a vehicle operator (Ghiselli, 1966). And so on. Here we are on the safe and uncontroversial ground of using tests as criterion samples. But this is a far cry from inferring that there is a general ability factor that enables a person to be more competent in anything he tries. The evidence for this general ability factor turns out to be contaminated heavily by the power of those at the top of the social hierarchy to insist that the skills they have are the ones that indicate superior adaptive capacity.

WHERE DO WE GO FROM HERE?

Criticisms of the testing movement are not new. The
Social Science Research Council Committee on Early
Identification of Talent made some of these same points
nearly fifteen years ago (McClelland, Baldwin, Bronfenbrenner, and Strodtbeck, 1958). But the beliefs on
which the movement is based are held so firmly that such
theoretical or empirical objections have had little impact
up to now. The testing movement continues to grow and
extend into every corner of our society. It is unlikely that
it can be simply stopped, although minority groups may
have the political power to stop it. For the tests are clearly
discriminatory against those who have not been exposed
to the culture, entrance to which is guarded by the tests.
What hopefully can happen is that testers will recognize
what is going on and attempt to redirect their energies in
a sounder direction. The report of the special committee
on testing to the College Entrance Examination Board
(1970) is an important sign that changes in thinking are
occurring—if only they can be implemented at a practical
level. The report's gist is that a wider array of talents
should be assessed for college entrance and reported as
a profile to the colleges. This is a step in the right direction if everyone keeps firmly in mind that the criteria for
establishing the "validity" of these new measures really
ought to be not *grades in school,* but "grades in life" in the
broadest theoretical and practical sense.

But now I am on the spot. Having criticized what the
testing movement has been doing, I feel some obligation
to suggest alternatives. How would I do things differently
or better? I do not mind making suggestions, but I am
well aware that some of them are as open to criticism on
other grounds as the procedures I have been criticizing.
So I must offer them in a spirit of considerable humility,

as approaches that at least some people might be interested in pursuing who are discouraged with what we have been doing. My goal is to brainstorm a bit on how things might be different, not to present hard evidence that my proposals are better than what has been done to date. How would one test for competence, if I may use that word as a symbol for an alternative approach to traditional intelligence testing?

1. THE BEST TESTING IS CRITERION SAMPLING.

The point is so obvious that it would scarcely be worth mentioning, if it had not been obscured so often by psychologists like McNemar and Jensen who tout a general intelligence factor. If you want to know how well a person can drive a car (the criterion), sample his ability to do so by giving him a driver's test. Do not give him a paper-and-pencil test for following directions, a general intelligence test, etc. As noted above, there is ample evidence that tests which sample job skills will predict proficiency on the job.

Academic skill tests are successful precisely because they involve criterion sampling for the most part. As already pointed out, the Scholastic Aptitude Test taps skills that the teacher is looking for and will give high grades for. No one could object if it had been recognized widely that this was *all* that was going on when aptitude tests were used to predict who would do well in school. Trouble started only when people assumed that these skills had some more general validity, as implied in the use of words like intelligence. Yet, even a little criterion analysis would show that there are almost no occupations or life situations that require a person to do word analogies, choose the most correct of four alternative meanings of a word, etc.

Criterion sampling means that testers have got to get out of their offices where they play endless word and paper-and-pencil games and into the field where they actually analyze performance into its components. If you want to test who will be a good policeman, go find out what a policeman does. Follow him around, make a list of his activities, and sample from that list in screening applicants. Some of the job sampling will have to be based on theory as well as practice. If policemen generally discriminate against blacks, that is clearly not part of the criterion because the law says that they must not. So include a test which shows the applicant does not discriminate. Also sample the vocabulary he must use to communicate with the people he serves since his is a position of interpersonal influence—and not the vocabulary that men who have never been on a police beat think it is proper to know. And do not rely on supervisors' judgments of who are the better policemen because that is not, strictly speaking, job analysis but analysis of what people think involves better performance. Baehr et al. (1968), for instance, found that black policemen in Chicago who were rated high by their superiors scored high on the Deference scale of the Edwards Personal Preference Test. No such relationship appeared for white policemen. In other words, if you wanted to be considered a good cop in Chicago and you were black, you had to at least talk as if you were deferent to the white power system. Any psychologist who used this finding to pick black policemen would be guilty of improper job analysis, to put it as mildly as possible.

Criterion sampling, in short, involves both theory and practice. It requires real sophistication. Early testers knew how to do it better than later testers because they had not become so caught up in the ingrown world of "intelligence" tests that simply were validated against each other. Testers of the future must relearn how to do criterion sampling. If someone wants to know who will make a good teacher, they will have to get videotapes of classrooms, as Kounin (1970) did, and find out how the behaviors of good and poor teachers differ. To pick future businessmen, research scientists, political leaders, prospects for a happy marriage, they will have to make careful behavioral analyses of these outcomes and then find ways of sampling the adaptive behavior in advance. The task will not be easy. It will require new psychological skills not ordinarily in the repertoire of the traditional tester. What is called for is nothing less than a revision of the role itself—moving it away from word games and statistics toward behavioral analysis.

2. TESTS SHOULD BE DESIGNED TO REFLECT CHANGES IN WHAT THE INDIVIDUAL HAS LEARNED.

It is difficult, if not impossible, to find a human characteristic that cannot be modified by training or experience, whether it be an eye blink or copying Kohs' block designs. To the traditional intelligence tester this fact has been something of a nuisance because he has been searching for some unmodifiable, unfakeable index of innate mental capacity. He has reacted by trying to keep secret the way his tests are scored so that people will not learn how to do them better, and by selecting tests, scores on which are stable from one administration to the next. Stability is supposed to mean that the score reflects an innate aptitude that is unmodified by experience, but it could also mean that the test is simply insensitive to important changes in what the person knows or can do. That is, the skill involved may be so specialized, so unrelated to general experience, that even though the person has learned a lot, he performs the same in this specialized area. For example, being able to play a word game like analogies is apparently little affected by a higher education, which is not so surprising since few teachers ask their students to do analogies. Therefore, being able to do analogies is often considered a sign of some innate ability factor. Rather, it might be called an achievement so specialized that increases in general wisdom do not transfer to it and cause changes in it. And why should we be interested in such specialized skills? As we have seen, they predictably do not seem to correlate with any life-outcome criteria except those that involve similar tests or that require the credentials that a high score on the test signifies.

It seems wiser to abandon the search for pure ability factors and to select tests instead that are valid in the sense that scores on them change as the person grows in experience, wisdom, and ability to perform effectively on various tasks that life presents to him. Thus, the second principle of the new approach to testing becomes a corollary of the first. If one begins by using as tests samples of life-outcome behaviors, then one way of determining whether those tests are valid is to observe that the person's ability to perform them increases as his competence in the life-outcome behavior increases. For example, if excellence in a policeman is defined partly in terms of being evenhanded toward all minority groups, then a test of fair-mindedness (or lack of ethnocentrism) might be used to select policemen and also should reflect growth in fairmindedness as a police recruit develops on the job. One of the hidden prejudices of psychology, borrowed from the notion of fixed inherited aptitudes, is that any trait, like racial prejudice, is unmodifiable by training. Once a bigot, always a bigot. There is no solid evidence that this trait or any other human trait cannot be changed. So it is worth insisting that a new test should be designed especially to reflect growth in the characteristic it assesses.

3. HOW TO IMPROVE ON THE CHARACTERISTIC TESTED SHOULD BE MADE PUBLIC AND EXPLICIT.

Such a principle contrasts sharply with present practice in which psychologists have tried hard—backed up by the

APA Ethics Committee—to keep answers to many of their tests a secret lest people practice and learn how to do better on them or fake high scores. Faking a high score is impossible if you are performing the criterion behavior, as in tests for reading, spelling, or driving a car. Faking becomes possible the more indirect the connection is between the test behavior and the criterion behavior. For example, in checking out hundreds of items for predicting flight training success, it may turn out that something like playing the piano as a boy has diagnostic validity. But no one knows exactly why: perhaps it has something to do with mechanical ability, perhaps with a social class variable, or with conscientiousness in practicing. The old-fashioned tester could not care less what the reason was as long as the item worked. But he had to be very careful about security because men who wanted to become pilots easily could report they had played the piano if they knew such an answer would help them be selected. If playing the piano actually helped people become better pilots—which no psychologist bothered to check out in World War II—then it might make some sense to make this known and encourage applicants to learn to play. That would be very like the criterion-sampling approach to testing proposed here, in which the person tested is told how to improve on the characteristic for which he will be tested.

Or to take another example, doing analogies is a task that predicts grades in school fairly well. Again no one knows quite why because schoolwork ordinarily does not involve doing analogies. So psychologists have had to be security conscious for fear that if students got hold of the analogies test answers, they might practice and become good at analogies and "fake" high aptitude. What is meant by faking here is that doing well on analogies is *not* part of the criterion behavior (getting good grades), or else it could hardly be considered faking. Rather, the test must have some indirect connection with good grades, so that doing well on it through practice destroys its predictive power: hence the high score is a "fake." The person can do analogies but that does not mean any longer that he will get better grades. Put this way, the whole procedure seems like a strange charade that testers have engaged in because they did not know what was going on, behaviorally speaking, and refused to take the trouble to find out as long as the items "worked." How much simpler it is, both theoretically and pragmatically, to make explicit to the learner what the criterion behavior is that will be tested. Then psychologist, teacher, and student can collaborate openly in trying to improve the student's score on the performance test. Certain school achievement tests, of course, follow this model. In the Iowa Test of Basic Skills, for instance, both pupil and teacher know how the pupil will be tested on spelling, reading, or arithmetic, how he should prepare for the test, how the tests will be scored, etc. What is proposed here is that *all* tests should follow this model. To do otherwise is to engage in power games with applicants over the secrecy of answers and to pretend knowledge of what lies behind correlations, which does not in fact exist.

4. TESTS SHOULD ASSESS COMPETENCIES INVOLVED IN CLUSTERS OF LIFE OUTCOMES.

If we abandon general intelligence or aptitude tests, as proposed, and move toward criterion sampling based on job analysis, there is the danger that the tests will become extremely specific to the criterion involved. For example, Project ABLE (Gagné, 1965) has identified over fifty separate skills that can be assessed for the exit level of millman apprentice (job family: woodworker and related occupations). They include skills like "measures angles," "sharpens tools and planes," and "identifies sizes and types of fasteners using gauges and charts." This approach has all of the characteristics of the new look in testing so far proposed: the tests are criterion samples; improvement in skill shows up in the tests; how to pass them is public knowledge; and both teacher and pupil can collaborate to improve test performance. However, what one ends up with is hundreds, even thousands, of specific tests for dozens of different occupations. For some purposes it may be desirable to assess competencies that are more generally useful in clusters of life outcomes, including not only occupational outcomes but social ones as well, such as leadership, interpersonal skills, etc. Project ABLE has been excellent at identifying the manual skills involved in being a service station attendant, but so far it has been unable to get a simple index of whether or not the attendant is pleasant to the customers.

Some of these competencies may be rather traditional cognitive ones involving reading, writing, and calculating skills. Others should involve what traditionally have been called personality variables, although they might better be considered competencies. Let me give some illustrations.

(a) *Communication skills.*   Many jobs and most interpersonal situations require a person to be able to communicate accurately by word, look, or gesture just what he intends or what he wants done. Writing is one simple way to test these skills. Can the person put together words in a way that makes immediate good sense to the reader? Word-game skills do not always predict this ability, as is often assumed. I will never forget an instance of a black student applicant for graduate school at Harvard who scored in something like the fifth percentile in the Miller Analogies Test, but who obviously could write and think clearly and effectively as shown by the stories he had written as a reporter in the college paper. I could not convince my colleagues to admit him despite the fact that he had shown the criterion behavior the Analogies Test is supposed to predict. Yet if he were admitted, as a psychologist, he would be writing papers in the future, not doing analogies for his colleagues. It is amazing to me how often my colleagues say things like: "I don't care how well he can write. Just look at those test scores." Testers may shudder at this, and write public disclaimers, but what practically have they done to stop the spread of this blind faith in test scores?

In Ethiopia in 1968 we were faced with the problem of trying to find out how much English had been learned by high school students who had been taught by American Peace Corps volunteers. The usual way of doing this there, as elsewhere, is to give the student a "fill in the blanks," multiple-choice objective test to see whether the student knows the meaning of words, understands correct grammatical forms, etc. We felt that this left out the most important part of the criterion behavior: the ability to use English to communicate. So we asked students to write brief stories which we then coded objectively, not for grammatical or spelling correctness, but for complexity of thought which the student was able to express correctly in the time allotted. This gave a measure of English fluency that predictably did correlate with occupational success among Ethiopian adults and also with school success, although curiously enough it was significantly negatively related to a word-game skill (English antonyms) that more nearly approximates the usual test of English competence (Bergthold, 1969).

Important communication skills are nonverbal. When the proverbial Indian said, "White man speak with forked tongue," he doubtless meant among other things that what the white man was saying in words did not jibe with what he was doing or expressing nonverbally. The abilities to know what is going on in a social setting and to set the correct emotional tone for it are crucial life-outcome criteria. Newmeyer (1970), for instance, has found a way to measure success at enacting certain emotions so that others receive them correctly and to measure success at receiving the correct emotions over various enactors. He found that black boys at a certain age were consistently better than white boys at this particular kind of communication skill, which is a far more crucial type of criterion behavior than most paper-and-pencil tests sample.

(b) *Patience.* Patience or response delay, as psychologists would call it, is a human characteristic that seems essential for many life outcomes. For instance, it is desirable for many service occupations where clients' needs and demands can be irritating. It would seem particularly desirable in a policeman who has the power and authority to do great damage to people who irritate him. Kagan, Pearson, and Welch (1966) have shown that it is an easily measured human characteristic that is relatively stable over time and can be taught directly.

(c) *Moderate goal setting.* This is important in achievement-related games, as I have explained fully elsewhere (McClelland, 1961). In most life situations, it is distinctly preferable to setting goals either too high or too low, which leads more often to failure. Many performance situations have been devised which measure the tendency to set moderate, achievable goals and help the person learn how to set more realistic goals in the future (Alschuler, Tabor, and McIntyre, 1970; McClelland and Winter, 1969).

(d) *Ego development.* Many scholars (see Erikson, 1950; Loevinger, 1970; White, 1959) have reasoned that there is a general kind of competence which develops with age and to a higher level in some people than in others. Costa (1971a) recently has developed a Thematic Apperception Test code for ego development which appears to have many of the aspects sought in the new measurement direction proposed here. The thought characteristics sampled represent criterion behavior in the sense that at Stage 1, for example, the person is thinking at a passive conformist level, whereas at Stage 4, he represents people in his stories as taking initiative on behalf of others (a more developed competency). The score on this measure predicts very well which junior or high school students will be perceived by their teachers as more competent (even when correlations with intelligence and grade performance are removed), and furthermore a special kind of education in junior high school moves students up the ego development scale significantly. That is, training designed to develop a sense of initiative produced results that were reflected sensitively in this score. Pupils and teachers can collaborate in increasing this kind of thinking which ought to prepare students for competent action in many spheres of life.

5. TESTS SHOULD INVOLVE OPERANT AS WELL AS
RESPONDENT BEHAVIOR.

One of the greatest weaknesses of nearly all existing tests is that they structure the situation in advance and demand a response of a certain kind from the test taker. They are aimed at assessing the capacity of a person to make a certain kind of response or choice. But life outside of tests seldom presents the individual with such clearly defined alternatives as "Which dog is most likely to bite?" or "Complete the following number series: 1 3 6 10 15 __," or "Check the word which is most similar in meaning to lexicon. . . ." If we refer to these latter behaviors as respondents in the sense that the stimulus situation clearly is designed to evoke a particular kind of response, then life is much more apt to be characterized by operant responses in the sense that the individual spontaneously makes a response in the absence of a very clearly defined stimulus. This fact probably explains why most existing tests do not predict life-outcome behaviors. Respondents generally do not predict operants. To use a crude example, a psychologist might assess individual differences in the *capacity* to drink beer, but if he used this measure to predict actual beer consumption over time, the chances are that the relationship would be very low. How much beer a person can drink is not related closely to how much he does drink.

Testers generally have used respondent behaviors to save time in scoring answers and to get higher test-retest reliability. That is, the person is more likely to give the same response in a highly structured situation than in an unstructured one that allows him to emit any behavior. Yet, slavishly pursuing these goals has led to important lacks in validity of the tests because life simply is not that structured, and often does not permit one to choose between defined-in-advance responses. The n Achievement measure, which is an operant in the sense that the subject emits responses (tells stories) under only very vague instructions, has predicted over a twelve-to-fourteen-year period in three different samples those who will drift into entrepreneurial business occupations (McClelland, 1965). Here an operant is predicting an operant—the tendency to think spontaneously about doing better all the time predicts a series of spontaneous acts over time which leads the individual into an entrepreneurial occupation. But predicting from operants to respondents or vice versa does not work, at least for men (McClelland, 1966). The n Achievement score is not related to grades or academic test scores (respondent measures), nor do grades relate to entering entrepreneurial occupations (see McClelland, 1961).

Even within fairly structured test situations it is possible to allow for more operant behavior than has been the usual practice. Not long ago we tried to find an existing performance test on which a person with high n Achievement ought to do well because such a test might be a useful substitute for the Thematic Apperception Test storytelling measure in certain situations. Theoretically, such a test should permit operant behavior in which the individual generates a lot of alternatives for solving a problem in search of the most efficient solution. But to our surprise we could find no such test. Tests of diver-

gent thinking existed that counted the number of operants (e.g., original uses for a paper clip) an individual
could come up with, but they did not require the person
to find the best alternative. Most other tests simply required the person to find the one correct answer the test
maker had built into the item. What was needed were test
items to which there were many correct answers, among
which one was better than others in terms of some criteria
of efficiency that the person would have to apply. This
task seemed more lifelike to us and certainly more like the
type of behavior characteristic of people with high n
Achievement. So we invented an Airlines Scheduling
Test (Bergthold, 1969) in which the person is faced with
a number of problems of getting a passenger from city A
to city B by such and such a time at minimum expenditure
in time, energy, money, and discomfort. From schedules
provided, several alternative routes and connections can
be generated (if the test taker is energetic enough to
think them up) that will solve the problem, but one is
clearly the most efficient. The test has promise in that it
correlates with the n Achievement score at a low level.
But the main point is that it requires more lifelike operant
behavior in generating alternative solutions and therefore it should have more predictive power to a variety of
situations in which what the person is expected to do is
not so highly structured as in standard respondent tests.

6. TESTS SHOULD SAMPLE OPERANT THOUGHT PATTERNS
TO GET MAXIMUM GENERALIZABILITY TO VARIOUS ACTION
OUTCOMES.

As noted already, the movement toward defining behavioral objectives in occupational testing can lead to great
specificity and huge inventories of small skills that have
little general predictive power. One way to get around
this problem is to focus on defining thought codes because, almost by definition, they have a wider range of

applicability to a variety of action possibilities. That is, they represent a higher order of behavioral abstraction than any given act itself which has not the capacity to stand for other acts the way a word does. And in empirical fact this is the way it has worked out. The n Achievement score—an operant thought measure—has many action correlates from goal setting and occupational styles to color and time-span preferences (McClelland, 1961) which individually have little power as "actones" to predict each other. A more recent example is provided by an operant thought measure of power motivation which has very low positive correlations with four action characteristics: drinking, gambling, accumulating prestige supplies, and confessing to having many aggressive impulses that are not acted on (McClelland, Davis, Kalin, and Wanner, 1972). These action characteristics are completely unrelated to each other so that they would be unlikely to come out on the same dimension in a factor analysis. But what is particularly interesting is that they appear to be alternative outlets for the power drive because the power motivation score correlates much higher with the maximum expression of *any one* of these alternatives than it does with any one alone or with the sum of standard scores on all of them. The thought characteristic—here the desire to "have impact," to make a big splash—is the higher order abstraction that gives the test predictive power for alternative ways of making a big splash in action—by gambling, drinking, etc. The tester of the future is likely to get farther in finding generalizable competencies of characteristics across life outcomes if he starts by focusing on thought patterns rather than by trying to infer what thoughts must lie behind the clusters of action that come out in various factors in the traditional trait analysis.

However, I have been arguing for this approach for over twenty years, and as far as I can see, the testing movement has been affected little by my eloquence.

Why? There are lots of reasons: People keep insisting that the n Achievement score is invalid because it will not predict grades in school—which is ironic since it was designed precisely to predict life outcomes and not grades in school. Or they argue it does not predict all types of achievement (Klinger, 1966)—when, of course, it is not supposed to, on theoretical grounds. But the practical problem (outside the tedium of content coding) is the unreliability of operant thought measures. Many of them are unreliable, though not all. Costa's (1971b) ego development score has a test-retest stability coefficient over a year of .66, $N = 223$. Unreliability is a fatal defect if the goal of testing is to *select* people, let us say, with high n Achievement. For rejected applicants could argue that they had been excluded improperly or that they might have high scores the next time they took the test, and the psychologist would have no good defense. One could just imagine beleaguered psychologists trying to defend themselves against irate parents whose children had not gotten into a preferred college because their n Achievement scores were too low.

But the emphasis in the new testing movement should be as much on evaluating educational progress as it is on identifying fixed characteristics for selection purposes. The operant thought measures are certainly reliable enough for the former objective. The educator can use them to assess whether a certain class or an innovative approach to teaching has tended, on the average, to promote ego development in thought as assessed by Costa's measure. The educator does not care *which particular child* is high in the measure since he does not plan to use the measure to select the child for special treatment. So its unreliability does not matter. He, as an administrator, can use the test information to decide whether the goals of the school are being forwarded by one educational approach or another. In a sense, the very unreliability of the thought measures may be a virtue if they encourage educators to stop thinking only about selection and start thinking more about evaluating educational progress.

Does this mean that test reliability is always unimportant? Not at all. Sometimes it will be important to diagnose deficiencies reliably that are to be made up. On other occasions tests will have to be used to pick out those most likely to be able to do a particular job well. So something will have to be done about reliability. Thus, a man with a high n Achievement score is a better bet for a sales job than a man with a low n Achievement score, but the measure of n Achievement from content coding of thought samples is not very defensible for selection purposes because it is unreliable. In this instance, the thought code can be used as the criterion against which more reliable performance measures can be validated. For example, the Airlines Scheduling Test score is reliable, and if it turns out to be related consistently to the n Achievement score based on thought sampling, it can be used as a substitute for the latter in selection. In fact, the thought codes can be considered devices for finding the clusters of action patterns that can be measured more reliably to get indexes of various competency domains central to various life outcomes. For example, if it turns out that an elevated socialized power (s Power) score (McClelland et al., 1972) characterizes successful policemen more than unsuccessful ones—as would be expected —then the action correlates of socialized power, such as capacity to lead or be influential in social groups, can be used to select potentially good policemen. The s Power score itself could not be so used because it is unreliable and "fakeable" if you learn the scoring system, but it is essential as a validating criterion for more reliable measures because its wide network of empirical and theoretical relationships helps find the action characteristics that will be useful for selection purposes.

While the six principles just enumerated for the new testing movement may affect occupational testing, the fact remains that testing has had its greatest impact in the schools and currently is doing the worst damage in that area by falsely leading people to believe that doing well in school means that people are more competent and therefore more likely to do well in life because of some real ability factor. Concretely, what would an organization like the Educational Testing Service do differently if it were to take these six principles into account? As a start, it might have to drop the term intelligence from its vocabulary and speak of scholastic achievement tests that are more or less content specific. The non-content-specific achievements (formerly called "aptitudes") do predict test-taking and symbol manipulation competencies, and these competencies are central to certain life-outcome criteria—like making up tests for others to pass or being proficient as a clerk (Ghiselli, 1966). But it is a serious practical and theoretical error to label them general intelligence, on the basis of evidence now available.

Once the innate intelligence philosophy is discarded, it becomes apparent that the role of such a testing service is to report to schools a profile of scholastic and non-scholastic achievements in a number of different areas. Then, in the case of selection, it is for the college to decide whether it has the educational programs that will promote growth in given areas of low performance. If performance is already high, say in mathematics, then the college probably can produce little improvement in that area and should ask itself in what other areas it can educate such a student, as shown by his lower levels of accomplishment at the outset. The profile particularly should include measures of such general characteristics as ego development or moral development (Kohlberg and Turiel, 1971) based on thought samples, because these general competencies ought to be improved by higher educational systems anyway.

The profile of achievements should be reported not only at entrance but at various points throughout the schooling to give teachers, administrators, and students feedback on whether growth in desired characteristics actually is occurring. Test results then become a device for helping students and teachers redesign the teaching-learning process to obtain mutually agreed-on objectives. Only then will educational testing turn from the sentencing procedure it now is into the genuine service it purports to be.

REFERENCES

ALSCHULER, A. S., TABOR, D., AND McINTYRE, J. *Teaching Achievement Motivation.* Middletown, Conn.: Educational Ventures, 1970.

ANDERSON, J. E. "The prediction of Adjustment Overtime," in *Personality Development in Children,* edited by I. Iscoe and H. Stevenson. Austin, Tex.: University of Texas Press, 1960.

BAEHR, M. E., FURCON, J. E., AND FROEMEL, E. C. *Psychological Assessment of Patrolman Gratifications in Relation to Field Performance.* Washington, D.C.: United States Government Printing Office, 1968.

BERG, I. *Education and Jobs: The Great Training Robbery.* New York: Praeger, 1970.

BERGTHOLD, G. D. "The Impact of Peace Corps Teachers on Students in Ethiopia." Ph.D. dissertation, Harvard University, 1969.

COLLEGE ENTRANCE EXAMINATION BOARD. *Report, Special Committee on Testing.* Princeton, N.J.: Educational Testing Service, 1970.

COSTA, P. "Introduction to the Costa Ego Development Manual." Department of Social Relations, Harvard University, 1971. (Mimeo) (a)

———"Working Papers on Ego Development Validation Research." Department of Social Relations, Harvard University, 1971. (Mimeo) (b)

CRONBACH, L. J. *Essentials of Psychological Testing.* 3rd ed. New York: Harper & Row, 1970.

ELTON, C. F., AND SHEVEL, L. R. *Who Is Talented? An Analysis of Achievement.* Res. rep. no. 31. Iowa City, Iowa: American College Testing Program, 1969.

ERIKSON, E. H. *Childhood and Society.* New York: Norton, 1950.

GAGNE, R. M. *The Conditions of Learning.* New York: Holt, Rinehart & Winston, 1965.

GHISELLI, E. E. *The Validity of Occupational Aptitude Tests.* New York: Wiley, 1966.

HAVIGHURST, R. J. et al. *Growing Up in River City.* New York: Wiley, 1962.

HOLLAND, J. L., AND RICHARDS, J. M., JR. *Academic and Nonacademic Accomplishment: Correlated or Uncorrelated?* Res. rep. no. 2. Iowa City, Iowa: American College Testing Program, 1965.

HOYT, D. P. *The Relationship between College Grades and Adult Achievement: A Review of the Literature.* Res. rep. no. 7. Iowa City, Iowa: American College Testing Program, 1965.

HUDSON, L. "Degree Class and Attainment in Scientific Research." *British Journal of Psychology* 51 (1960): 67–73.

JENSEN, A. R. "The Heritability of Intelligence." *Saturday Evening Post* 244, no. 2 (1972): 9, 12, 149.

KAGAN, J., PEARSON, L., AND WELCH, L. "The Modifiability of an Impulsive Tempo." *Journal of Educational Psychology* 57: 1966): 359–365.

KENT, D. A., AND EISENBERG, T. "The Selection and Promotion of Police Officers." *The Police Chief,* February 1972, pp. 20–29.

KLINGER, E. "Fantasy Need Achievement as a Motivational Construct." *Psychological Bulletin* 66 (1966): 291–308.

KOHLBERG, L., LACROSSE, J., AND RICKS, D. "The Predictability of Adult Mental Health from Childhood Behavior." In *Handbook of child psychopathology,* ed. B. Wolman. New York: McGraw-Hill, 1970.

KOHLBERG, L., AND TURIEL, E. *Moralization Research: The Cognitive Development Approach.* New York: Holt, Rinehart & Winston, 1971.

KOUNIN, J. S. *Discipline and Group Management in Classrooms.* New York: Holt, Rinehart & Winston, 1970.

LOEVINGER, J., AND WESSLER, R. *Measuring Ego Development.* 2 vols. San Francisco: Jossey-Bass, 1970.

McCLELLAND, D. C. *The Achieving Society.* New York: Van Nostrand-Rheinhold, 1961.

———"*N* Achievement and Entrepreneurship: A Longitudinal Study." *Journal of Personality and Social Psychology* 1 (1965): 398–392.

———"Longitudinal Trends in the Relation of Thought to Action." *Journal of Consulting Psychology* 30 (1966): 479–483.

———"Education for Competence." In *Proceedings of the 1971 FOLEB Conference,* ed. H. Heckhausen and W. Edelstein. Berlin, Germany: Institut für Bildungsforschung in der Max-Planck-Gesellschaft, in press.

————, BALDWIN, A. L., BRONFENBRENNER, U., AND STRODTBECK, F. L. *Talent and Society.* Princeton, N.J. Van Nostrand, 1958.

————, DAVIS, W. N., KALIN, R., AND WANNER, H. E. *The Drinking Man.* New York: Free Press, 1972.

————AND WINTER, D. G. *Motivating Economic Achievement.* New York: Free Press, 1969.

MCNEMAR, Q. "Lost: Our Intelligence? Why?" *American Psychologist* 19 (1964): 871–882.

NEWMEYER, J. A. "Creativity and Nonverbal Communication in Preadolescent White and Black Children." Ph.D. dissertation, Harvard University, 1970.

NUTTALL, R. L., AND FOZARD, T. L. "Age, Socioeconomic Status and Human Abilities." *Aging and Human Development* 1 (1970): 161–169.

TAYLOR, C., SMITH, W. R., AND GHISELIN, B. "The Creative and Other Contributions of One Sample of Research Scientists." In *Scientific Creativity: Its Recognition and Development,* ed. C. W. Taylor, and F. Barron. New York: Wiley, 1963.

TERMAN, L. M., AND ODEN, M. H. *The Gifted Child Grows Up.* Stanford, Calif.: Stanford University Press, 1947.

THORNDIKE, R. L. AND HAGEN, E. *10,000 Careers.* New York: Wiley, 1959.

WECHSLER, D. *The Measurement and Appraisal of Adult Intelligence.* 4th ed. Baltimore, Md.: Williams & Wilkins, 1958.

WHITE, R. W. "Motivation Reconsidered: The Concept of Competence." *Psychological Review* 66 (1959): 297–333.

WING, C. W., JR., AND WALLACH, M. A. *College Admissions and the Psychology of Talent.* New York: Holt, Rinehart & Winston, 1971.

The Trap of Environmentalism

STANLEY ARONOWITZ

Liberal humanists (those who oppose inequality but refuse to locate its sources in the social structure) are mobilizing their intellectual and political forces to combat what *Social Policy* has characterized as the "new assault on equality." This assault has taken many forms and seems to emanate from several directions. The most discussed, the attempt by Arthur Jensen and Richard Herrnstein[1] to revive the idea that a close correlation exists between heredity and intelligence, and that blacks are demonstrably inferior to whites when measured by IQ tests, has drawn the fire of all those deeply committed to racial equality. But the critics of genetic explanations have sought to make their case in environmental terms. Whatever may be the cultural or genetic inheritance of any group, liberal humanists seem to have no choice but to focus on the environment. For example, they point out that it is impossible to measure intelligence objectively. "There are no tests of native intelligence. In fact, the concept of native intelligence is essentially meaning-

SOURCE: Stanley Aronowitz, "The Trap of Environmentalism," *Social Policy* 3, no. 3 (September-October 1972).

1. Arthur R. Jensen, "How Much Can We Boast IQ and Scholastic Achievement?" *Harvard Educational Review* 39 (Winter 1969): 1–123; Richard Herrnstein, "IQ," *Atlantic* September, 1971.

less."[2] All the IQ test measures is the probable performance of children in schools as presently constructed. Or they contend that schools presume a certain cultural orientation by students and have developed norms that accord with this orientation. There are no tests that measure the capacity of black children to survive in the everyday life of the ghetto, they point out. The intelligence needed to live in a way radically different from the dominant American culture is of no concern to the dominant society. (On the other hand, the few attempts to devise "culture-free" tests are simply not as effective in predicting school achievement.)

The problem with the environmentalist rebuttal to genetic determinism is, however, that they are fighting on their so-called enemy's terrain. Despite their serious differences with those identified as conservatives, the liberal critics who assert their adherence to equality are constrained by their own acceptance of the prevailing social division of labor—and the role of IQ measures, public schools, and merit within it. Too often they share the conservative belief that incremental changes can remedy the illnesses of society and only differ with them about the pace and extent of these changes. But even when this is not the case, the liberal egalitarians' environmentalist defense against the kind of genetic assertions presented by Arthur Jensen continually concedes the upper hand to the opposition. The fact is that genetic theories of the performance of groups in society carry with them the force of real social arrangements.

The very category of measurable intelligence itself implies a social order that requires it. We need to alter the presuppositions and change the fulcrum of debate when we are talking seriously about modifying and eradicating

2. "Education, Ethnicity, Genetics and Intelligence," *IRCD Bulletin* 5, no. 4 (1969). Publication of the ERIC Information Retrieval Center on the Disadvantaged.

socially bred inequities. Environmentalists are diverted by a false dichotomy. To be sure, there are both environmental and innate aspects to the development of any aspect of human activity. (The person is not merely the sum of social forces that shape him or her.) But the defensive polarity of environmentalism diverts our attention from the ways children of different classes, races, and sexes are taught and from the introjection of socially determined attitudes of inferiority among those who can expect to remain powerless, propertyless, and oppressed all of their lives. This internalization of failure is not groundless.

In addition to considering intelligence as a factor in learning, we have to consider what is to be learned, by whom, and for what purpose. If the object of education is to provide a labor force for the existing social structure with its hierarchical division of social labor, then there is good reason to expect black children and working-class children to fail. Economic and social power in the United States and all advanced industrial countries is built on a pyramidal configuration. There is no room at the top. The mobility achieved by working-class people through education is normally confined to movement from unskilled to skilled manual labor, and to the expanding number of niches in industries and occupations where the manipulation of symbols rather than things constitutes the substance of work.

The IQ test, around which so much of the equality debate rages, was devised as a screening process to assist schools and industry to rationalize the prevailing social divisions of labor on a scientific basis and to determine which children shall occupy the various economic niches within the social order. The test made its appearance a few years before World War I, when the United States was beginning to exhibit the same economic stagnation and rigidity of class structure as its European counterparts. The importance of the IQ was that it reinforced the myth of a meritocracy, the only viable ideology for a society that teaches its children that there are no classes and proclaims adherence to the doctrine of equality. The individual's failure to rise is attributed to his or her inability or unwillingness to seize the unlimited opportunities available to the energetic, intelligent, or talented.

The IQ test symbolizes America's interpretation of equality to mean equality of opportunity. Emphasis on equality of opportunity has meant trying to make it possible for the poor to become less poor by encouraging them to overcome the environmental pressures on them. In this context environmentalists implicitly assume the standards set by the standardized IQ measure—namely, access to a job as reward, not access to a more powerful participation in determining how the pie is to be divided. By assuming this objective uncritically, the environmentalist legitimized the view that poor people—and black poor people in particular—have capitulated to negative environmental conditions. This left two options: help them or give up on them. They had to earn their rights by proving themselves in the existing mainstream. The obligation of the mainstream was to try to make this possible. In effect, then, the environmentalist position tended to confirm the system, calling for its expansion to include more people who earned their place by the merit teased out of them; it failed to question the normative basis of a system with relative future, and absolute future, built into it. It said that the system (by its favorite measures) were selecting out too many people for its own good. The environmentalists did not say opportunity should be an outgrowth of inalienable human rights, instead of an anvil to which more people must be led and tested on.

The development of the IQ test coincided with the effort to make compulsory public education responsive to the tremendous advances of technology accompanying the industrial revolution in late nineteenth-century

American capitalism. Free public education was a way to deal with the superfluity of child labor as well as the demands of the new techniques being introduced in American industry. The public schools became a vast container for children who were no longer needed in the factories and a mechanism for socializing appropriate industrial employee behavior. Despite the humanistic purposes of many educators, the schools served the need of the economic order for a labor force preselected according to criteria that place responsibility on the individual to perform in conformity with standards of behavior and intelligence determined from above.

And what of those standards? Instead of the critical thinking and personal autonomy with which the rhetoric of schooling has been padded, intelligence tests have been a perfect instrument for the selection of people possessing characteristics best suited to conformity in bureaucratically organized systems. [3]

Indeed, a good case could be made that IQ tests really inversely measure authentic problem-solving intelligence and reason; that doing well on these tests implies a trained incapacity to think in depth, to think innovatively, to be creative.

Meanwhile, the possibility of upward mobility for all Americans has remained a powerful ideology—for liberals, conservatives, as well as for the victims of this society for whom the promises perenially prove false. The fight for civil rights was a fight for the access other minority groups appeared to have achieved. This program, like the myths underpinning it, seemed viable as long as the economy was expanding, especially in those sectors requiring new workers, such as the public sector. And even then not all places were equal. But in the late 1960s it became evident to many black militants that the political

3. Erich Fromm, *Man for Himself* (New York: Rinehart, 1947), p. 75.

economy was only admitting blacks into the working class; genuine mobility seemed a long way off. At the same time second-generation white workers began to perceive that their fate was circumscribed by conditions of birth. That is, young workers were sharing the fate of their fathers, with the notable exception that, while their fathers were employed largely in manual occupations, many youth were being squeezed by a tight white or gray collar.

The liberals are in a quandary because they have accepted the equation of equality with equality of opportunity; they, and the upwardly mobile masses of less fortunate Americans who hoped with them, confused access to jobs with access to power. Therefore, when the social and occupational structure provides little room for movement, there is only frustration. One clear possible direction is to abandon the superficial concepts of the environment inherited from the nineteenth century. The social environment is, first, the class structure within which the production of goods and services takes place. Second, it is in the hierarchically arranged strata within the class structure that perpetuate and reinforce doctrines of inequality. By accepting the prevailing social divisions of labor—that is, the distinctions based on mental and physical labor, seniority, presumed skill levels, and credentials—liberals cannot combat distinctions based on race and sex, which are functions of the larger social structure. Women may enter the professions or blacks may find their way into managerial posts within the public sector, but these token advances accorded to "meritorious" members of the sex or race have nothing to do with real political or social power; nor do they alter materially the inequality of the larger system. The only way to advance the reality of equality is to examine the way in which the social system is organized, to develop a critique of the concept of authority and hierarchially determined role differences, distinguishing between the divisions necessitated by technological criteria and those determined by bureaucratic and authoritarian criteria.

The distribution of power in America remains unaltered despite "equality of opportunity." The concentration and centralization of capital has increased the power a few large corporate groups exert over American society. The intermeshing of corporate leadership and the government has become more complete in the past thirty years, owing to the necessity for large-scale government intervention in the economy in order to maintain a modicum of economic stability. The government's power, but not its autonomy, has been enlarged as a result of its new functions. It has been colonized by the corporations, who choose periodically to surrender their autonomy to the government when there are differences between them, as long as they are certain that the state represents their general interests. We are witnessing an erosion of pluralistic political ideology. The difference between the national state and other crucial institutions of social cohesion is diminishing. Trade unions, educational institutions, health institutions, and local governments are all dependent on the coordinating apparatus of the state for their sustenance. Moreover, the slowing down of economic growth constitutes a barrier to the perpetuation of the doctrine of merit, according to which all groups have equal access to occupational mobility through education. The manifest surplus of highly credentialed workers has created new tasks for corporate-minded theorists.

If all this is true then the concept of equality must come under attack from all sides: from the frustrated, from the disappointed, and from those for whom it has been a useful but insincere persuasion. The recourse to theories of genetic determinism makes perfect sense unless a new theory arises that discounts the illusory classlessness of this society and the supposed leveling function of the schools. The present impact of Jensen and Herrnstein (scientists provided similar studies in the 1940s and 1950s) must be interpreted in the context of shrinking employment opportunities and the strength of the hierarchical organization and division of labor in this society. Furthermore, the present resurgence of discussion about IQ tests must also be seen within the context of other arguments for genetic determinism. Arguments for a genetically determined IQ stem from the same sources as arguments for the "instinctual" basis of aggression, for the chromosomal basis of criminality, or for the physiological and biochemical basis for differences between men and women in their ability to "bond" and form political association.[4] We are witnessing the resurgence of dormant aspects of a conventional wisdom geared to competitive scarcity in response to strains and stresses of a system characterized by these terms. Recall what Marx said in *The German Ideology:* "The ruling ideas are nothing more than the ideal expression of the dominant natural relationships, the dominant material relationships grasped as ideas." The same holds true today, both as analysis and as a focus for action.

4. Konrad Lorenz, *On Aggression* (New York: Bantam Books, 1967); Robert Audrey, *African Genesis* (New York: Dell, 1963). Audrey's later books also uphold this view, although in increasingly modified form. See also Lionel Tiger, *Men in Groups* (New York: Random House, 1969).

The Hidden IQ*

FRANK RIESSMAN

Intelligence tests measure how quickly people can solve relatively unim-portant problems making as few errors as possible, rather than measuring how people grapple with relatively important problems, making as many productive errors as necessary with time no factor.†

A few years ago a birthday party for a member of the staff at a well-known psychological clinic played a novel role in the test performance of a Negro child. Prior to the party this boy, whom we shall call James, had been de-scribed on the psychological record as "sullen, surly, slow, unresponsive, apathetic, unimaginative, lacking in inner life." This description was based on his behavior in the clinic interviews and on his performance on a number of psychological measures including an intelligence test and a personality test. His was not an unusual record; many culturally deprived children are similarly por-trayed.

On the day of the birthday party, James was seated in

SOURCE: Frank Riessman, "The Hidden IQ," in *The Culturally Deprived Child* (New York: Harper and Row, 1962). Reprinted by permission of the publisher.

*In this chapter we are particularly indebted to Walter Murray for permitting us to quote from his unpublished paper, "Some Major Assumptions Underlying the Development of Intelligence Tests," 1960.

†Personal communication to the author from Irving Taylor.

an adjoining room waiting to go into the clinician's office. It was just after the lunch hour, and James had the first afternoon appointment. The conclusion of the lunch break on this particular day was used by the staff to present a surprise birthday cake to one of the clinicians who happened to be a Negro. The beautifully decorated cake was brought in and handed to the recipient by James's clinician who was white, as were all the other members of the staff. The Negro woman was deeply moved by the cake—and the entire surprise. In a moment of great feeling, she warmly embraced the giver of the cake. James inadvertently perceived all this from his vantage point in the outer office. That afternoon he showed amazing alacrity in taking the tests and responding in the interview. He was no longer sullen and dull. On the contrary, he seemed alive, enthusiastic, and he answered questions readily. His psychologist was astonished at the change and in the course of the next few weeks retested James on the tests on which he had done so poorly. He now showed marked improvement, and she quickly revised not only the test appraisal of him on the clinical record card, but her general personality description of him as well.

The high point of their new, positive relationship came some months later when he confided to her that she had gotten off on the wrong foot with him on the first day in the first three minutes of contact. She was taken aback and said, "What do you mean? I was very friendly, I told you my name and asked you yours." He responded, "Yeh, and I said James Watson and right away you called me Jimmy and you bin callin' me Jimmy ever since. My name is James, 'cept to my very good friends maybe. Even my mother calls me James." Then he went on to tell her how he had changed his opinion of her on the day of the birthday party because of the close relationship he had seen widened between her and the Negro psychologist.

This little story illustrates a number of things. First, it shows that *the test is a social situation.* The testing situation, whether it be a psychological test or any other kind of test, for that matter, reflects a relationship between people, a relationship that is often remarkably subtle. And when anything hampers this relationship, the result is likely to show in the test score itself. This can occur on an individual test as well as a group test, an IQ test as well as a personality test, a subject matter examination as well as a psychological measure.

It also shows how the behavior evidenced in the clinical situation tends to be seen by the psychologist as indicative of the basic personality of the child. This is frequently done with little awareness of how much this behavior is a product of the particular relationship of the psychologist to the child, and of the testing situation as such. Children from different cultural backgrounds respond very differently to clinical situations and to the idea of being tested or evaluated.

The anecdote also points up the fact that a well-meaning, clinically trained, unprejudiced psychologist can have poor rapport with a deprived child, not because of deficient psychological technique, but because of limited knowledge about certain cultural attitudes. In this case, the attitude in question is the feeling held by many Negro people that the informality intended by shortened nicknames signifies a lack of respect when it takes place across cultural lines. This does not suggest that the child himself was aware of this reasoning, but that, rather, he was simply reflecting his parents' wish that he be called by his full name.

The importance of having Negro psychologists on the staff of a clinic is shown in a pertinent way by the anecdote. The Negro child need not himself have a Negro clinician, but her presence in the clinic was indirectly influential.

Finally, the story neatly illustrates the fact that scores on tests are not fixed and can be reversed dramatically when the relationship to the tester is improved. There is apparently a hidden IQ and a hidden personality that is often not revealed by the test and the clinical interview. In our story, James's IQ score rose considerably in the retesting and his personality began to appear in a totally new light.

THE IQ CONTROVERSY

Currently there is considerable questioning of some of the basic assumptions of the IQ test. Consistent with the incident we have just reported, the old notion that the IQ is relatively stable or constant is under heavy fire. There is increasing recognition that IQ scores of under-privileged children do not reflect their ability, because the test items include words that are not in the experience repertoire of these children.

But there are many other assumptions involved that have not been as fully questioned, and perhaps it would be a good idea to briefly trace the history of the IQ controversy.

At first the issue revolved around whether the lower IQ of deprived children was a result of heredity or environment. Research indicated that environmental factors were apparently decisive in producing the higher middle-class IQ. Then Allison Davis questioned the applicability of the IQ tests to deprived groups.[1] He wondered if the tests might not be impregnated with middle-class prob-lems and language, and thus not be fair to under-privileged youngsters.

What Davis did was to take various intelligence test problems on which the deprived did poorly, and reword them in terms equally familiar to all children. For exam-ple:

1. Allison Davis, *Social-Class Influences Upon Learning* (Cam-bridge Mass.: Harvard University Press, 1948).

Instead of "Cub is to bear as gosling is to 1( ) fox, 2( ) grouse, 3 ( ) goose, 4 ( ) rabbit, 5 ( ) duck," he substituted, "Puppy goes with dog like kitten goes with 1 ( ) fox, 2 ( ) goose, 3 ( ) cat, 4 ( ) rabbit, 5 ( ) duck."

The required understanding of the relationship of the concepts is not altered by the revised form. If the child does not know the word "gosling," he can never demonstrate his grasp of the relationship required in this question. In other words, until the change was made, this item was functioning as a vocabulary test for the disadvantaged child.[2] The reformulation changed not only the vocabulary involved, but also the structure of the sentence to read "puppy *goes with* dog like kitten *goes with*——." "Goes with" is substituted for "is to." This made the problem more understandable to the underprivileged children.

Surprisingly enough, however, even though Davis's changes produced a test that was more attuned to them, disadvantaged youngsters did not improve markedly. Something else apparently was deterring them. It remained for Ernest Haggard to clear up the mystery.[3]

2. Robert Havighurst, one of Davis's colleagues, points out that items requiring knowledge of the following words may touch the experience of the middle-class child but not that of the deprived child: fireplace, chandelier, wall-paper, salad fork, dining room. Words which might be more familiar to deprived children, such as pump, coal stove, kerosene lamp, rain barrel, rarely appear on intelligence tests. Kenneth Eels et al., *Intelligence and Cultural Differences* (Chicago: University of Chicago Press, 1951), p. 18.

3. Ernest A. Haggard, "Social Status and Intelligence," in *Genetic Psychology Monographs* 49, (1954): pp. 141–186; also personal communications from Dr. Haggard.

THE BIG THREE: PRACTICE, MOTIVATION, RAPPORT

Haggard reasoned that although deprived children may have taken many IQ tests, they really did not know how to take these tests properly: they lacked meaningful, directed practice. They also lacked motivation, and their relationship to the examiner was typically distant and beset by fears.

Haggard decided to control each of these factors. He gave both deprived and nondeprived children three one-hour training periods in taking IQ tests. These practice periods included careful explanation of what was involved in each of the different types of problems found on the IQ tests. The explanations were given in words that were familiar to both groups. Haggard also offered special rewards for doing well, and he trained his examiners to be responsive to the deprived children as well as to the middle-class youngsters, thus greatly enhancing the rapport.[4]

4. In the area of motivation, it is clear that middle-class children are more motivated to do well on examinations of the IQ sort because of the general emphasis on success and competition in middle-class life. Even where an examination is not directly related to a reward or a threat, the middle-class child strives to perform well. Part of the difference in IQ scores of middle-class and deprived children is due to differences in strength of motivation to perform well on an examination rather than to differences in intelligence.

This point is indirectly verified in a study by Douvan. At first, an examination was given to both deprived and middle-class youngsters without any indication of its importance, or of an offering of a meaningful reward for satisfactory work. The result was typical: the middle-class group showed far greater motivation than the deprived group. Later, the test was rerun, but this time a reward was offered for successful work on the test. The result: the motivation of the deprived group increased much

Under these conditions the IQs of the disadvantaged children improved sharply. *This occurred with only three hours of practice.*[5] And it occurred even on the old IQ tests with the middle-class-biased items. Apparently more important than the content of the test items was the attitude of the children toward the test situation and the examiner.

Haggard also showed that when test items were read aloud to the deprived children while they followed in their test booklets, these children did much better.[6] Deprived children are notoriously poor readers. Consequently, their typically inadequate intelligence test performance is partly a result of that difficulty rather than of limited intelligence.

It might be asked at this point, why all the fuss—if deprived children cannot read well, what difference does it make if we say they are less intelligent, or that they are deficient in reading? The answer is that it makes a huge difference because of the contrasting implications of deficiencies in intelligence and deficiencies in reading ability. Reading skill, it is generally accepted, can be improved fairly easily, certainly in the child, and to some degree even in the adult, where motivation is present. On the other hand, the old assumption was that intelligence, while it is affected by experience and knowledge, is much less easily changed or improved. Perhaps not much can be done in schools to help deprived children if they suffer

---

more than that of the middle-class group. Thus, when the test situation promised rewards that were direct, immediate, practical, and meaningful, deprived children responded at a higher level than where such rewards were absent. But less so with middle-class youth, who are more often motivated to perform at close to their maximum level even while rewards are absent. See Elizabeth Douvan, "Social Status and Success Striving," *Journal of Abnormal and Social Psychology*, March 1956, pp. 219–223.

5. Haggard, "Social Status and Intelligence."
6. Ibid.

from low intelligence; but the outlook is much more positive if the problem is poor reading.*

IQ ASSUMPTIONS DISCRIMINATE AGAINST THE DEPRIVED

Walter Murray, one of Davis's coworkers, is currently
continuing the analysis of basic assumptions underlying
the IQ. He questions the following assumptions which
function either directly or indirectly to penalize the deprived child: [7]

1. The IQ is measured by the use of brief exercises that
have to be executed fairly quickly; while "many of the
problems that individuals are expected to solve in real life
require much time and concentration," this type of task
is excluded from the IQ test.

The brief exercises and the general accent on speed in

*It might be objected, of course, that in Haggard's investiga-
tion the underprivileged youngsters improved more than did the
middle-class because the latter had the higher IQ scores and
thus could not improve upon them. There are two answers to
this objection, one of which is somewhat technical: Haggard
points out that through the use of a special statistical method
(the Johnson-Neyman technique), the effect of the higher IQ of
the middle-class children was held constant or removed. (Haggard, personal communication)

Secondly, and less technical, the argument overlooks a fundamental assumption underlying most intelligence tests, namely,
that the IQ is relatively stable, and that it certainly *cannot be raised
easily.* Haggard's study shows, on the contrary, that in a period
of five days that included only three one-hour practice sessions,
the IQ of large numbers of deprived youngsters could be significantly increased. What seems to be involved here is that if the
individual or group is not functioning with high motivation, or
if efficient test-taking techniques have not been developed, or if
rapport with the examiner is not good, the resulting *performance*
can rather readily be improved.

7. Murray, "Intelligence Tests."

particular work against the deprived child. His style is
slow and cautious. It takes him a long time to become
involved in problems, and his potential will not easily be
evidenced on short, speed-oriented tasks. He will, in all
likelihood, show his ability only after he is absorbed in a
problem. Many nondeprived children have a similar work
orientation, of course, and rural children find the speed
emphasis equally distasteful.

Allison Davis notes that speed is affected by cultural
attitudes concerning the importance or unimportance of
speed, and by personality factors, such as "competitive-
ness, conscientiousness, compulsiveness, exhibitionism,
and anxiety."[8] *These personality characteristics are less frequently associated with the deprived child's personality pattern.*

2. The IQ score is based on the accuracy of the final
answer to the IQ question, not the method of thinking
involved in arriving at this answer. "In most tests the final
score, or judgment of the student's intelligence, is based
on the number of correct responses. Little or no attention is given to the method by which the student attacked
the problem or the kinds of considerations he made use
of in attempting to solve it."[9]

The deprived child does not possess, as one psychologist put it recently, "good avoidance conditioning for

8. Ibid.
9. Haggard reports the following:

In one study, children were asked to give the reasons for
their answers to intelligence test items. In the case of one
analogy item, 35 of the 60 children tested marked the "correct" response, but not one of these children gave the "correct" reason for marking it. The reasons given were on the
basis of rhyming, synonym, etc., but not on the basis of
making the analogy—the process which the test constructor
assumed was being measured.

Ernest A. Haggard, "Techniques for the Development of
Unbiased Tests," *Proceedings: 1952 Conference on Testing Problems*
(Princeton, N. J.: Educational Testing Service, 1953).

wrong answers." He does not have a good sense for what is likely to be a poor answer because he has limited test-taking skills. The teacher and the psychologist are typically oriented toward getting the right answer, and are less interested in the thinking processes involved, particularly when this thinking does not lead to the correct result.[10]

3. Intelligence is assumed to develop and increase with age; items which do not show an improvement with age are excluded from the IQ tests.

The assumption that intelligence increases with age has an indirect effect on the measurement of the IQ of the deprived child. Characteristically his measured IQ has been found to *fall* with age. This is, apparently, because he has not been exposed to the experiences and vocabulary presumed to be normal in the culture, and on which all the IQ tests are based. Now if it were possible to have IQ exercises that were not dependent on these experiences, and that measured skills that did not improve with the age of the child, the underprivileged child might fare better.

4. It is assumed that intelligence is best demonstrated in a school environment. IQ tests have tended to become tests of scholastic aptitude. Intelligence may be relatively

---

10. Haggard reports a study in which:

"The test constructor wrote out the mental processes he thought were being measured by the items in his published test. It was found that for some items over 50 percent of the 152 nine- and ten-year-old children gave logically defensible reasons for marking answers considered "incorrect" by the test constructor. Furthermore, whenever more than one logically defensible answer to an item was given, the middle-class children tended to give the "correct" answer (in the opinion of the test constructor), whereas lower-class children tended to give the "incorrect" answer (in the opinion of the test constructor).

Ibid.

unimportant in business, industry, agriculture, etc., but this does not on the surface appear to be a very sound assumption.

With regard to the highly academic character of the IQ test, Ralph Tyler notes:

... so far as problem-solving exercises are concerned the typical intelligence tests lean heavily on academic, school-type problems, whereas lower-class children frequently have had more experience than have middle-class children in dealing with the kinds of practical problems encountered on the street and in the playground. That is to say, it seems clear . . . that youngsters who do not show up well on intelligence tests do possess abilities that indicate some skill in solving practical problems and that suggest potentialities for further education if the schools had broad enough goals to utilize talents of these kinds.[11]

EARLY ENVIRONMENT AND THE CHANGEABILITY OF THE IQ

Few people still maintain the old assumption that the IQ is necessarily stable or constant throughout life. There is too much evidence showing that it can be changed under varying conditions. But an allied view has been advanced that is related to the "constancy" assumption.

This argument holds that the underprivileged child has been immersed in an early "impoverished" environment in which there is insufficient stimulation, thus producing a *basic retardation*, so that, in effect, his IQ remains relatively low throughout life.[12]

11. Ralph W. Tyler, "Can Intelligence Tests Be Used to Predict Educability," in *Intelligence and Cultural Differences*, Kenneth Eells et al. (Chicago: University of Chicago Press, 1951), p. 43.
12. Donald Hebb, a leading psychologist, makes the assumption that the early childhood period is of decisive importance in

One version of this argument maintains that the early environment of the deprived child produces behavior similar to that sometimes found in institutional children, and in children brought up in isolation from society. At its extreme, this view sees the behavior of deprived children as being similar to that found in the stimulus deprivation experiments, where volunteers are put in special respiratory tanks for twenty-four hours. (Following these experiments, the subjects are unable to concentrate, their IQ performance and problem-solving ability temporarily deteriorates, and they are in a general fog.) The stimulus deprivation thesis presumes that the underprivileged child has suffered some similar lack of stimulation over a long period of time, particularly in his early life, and that this accounts for his low IQ. There are three levels at which this argument may be challenged:

1. In the first place, the stimulus-depriving tank analogy seems extremely far-fetched because, whatever one may say about the environment of these children, it certainly is not lacking in stimulation per se. Witness the crowded homes and streets, the noise, parties, TV sets, the sports, games, fights, etc.

2. Moreover, the family life includes a good deal of sibling interaction, physical punishment, definite toilet training, masturbation inhibition, breast feeding, and various responsibility demands. Regardless of the particular evaluation one may wish to place on these practices, they do appear to provide stimulation. This environment

determining later intelligence. He believes that Negro and poor white children have had insufficient stimulation in their early development, and that this accounts for their lower *functioning* intelligence at a later age. He accepts the intelligence test performance as an accurate indicator of operating intelligence although he believes it to be a completely inaccurate index of *capacity*—inherent intelligence. See Donald O. Hebb, *Organization of Behavior* (New York: Wiley, 1949), chap. 2.

seems quite distinct from that of children reared in isolation from society.

3. Haggard's findings further call into question the inference concerning "basic retardation," because if the IQ can be so markedly improved by only three hours of special training, surely the childhood experiences cannot have been so limiting or irreversible. It might also be added that much of the behavior of deprived children, in nonacademic spheres, gives evidence of considerable spontaneity, a trait not ordinarily associated with a history of deficient stimulation.

CREATIVITY AND THE IQ

Erich Fromm comments on intelligence tests that "they measure not so much the capacity for reason and understanding as the capacity for quick mental adaptation to a given situation; 'mental adjustment tests' would be the adequate name for them."[13]

The items used on the tests do not require any intrinsic interest or curiosity on the part of the subject. On the contrary, if he becomes too interested in any one item he will probably take too much time on it and possibly give an unconventional response that might be marked as being wrong. The motivation called for on the test is not interest in the specific questions as such, but rather an overall competitive motivation to do well. But the intelligence of certain kinds of people may not really be tapped unless they are deeply involved in the specific problem on which they are working. This is more likely to be the case with disadvantaged individuals.

Psychologists have come to disagree with the notion that a high IQ is the mark of "giftedness" or creativity.

13. Erich Fromm, *Man for Himself* (New York: Rinehart, 1947), p. 75.

Dr. Westcott[14] at Vassar College has developed a specific test for measuring creativity that has been validated in terms of actual creative accomplishments of the students —accomplishments such as writing a piece of music, poetry, and the like. He finds little relationship between creativity and IQ scores.[15]

The IQ of deprived individuals is generally relatively low but their creativity is often shown in nonacademic ways: A prominent labor union economist, Solomon Bar-

14. Malcolm R. Westcott, "A Method for the Study of Creativity as a Special Case of Problem Solving," (Paper presented at the Eastern Psychological Association, New York City, April 16, 1960).

15. An article in *New York Times*, February 18, 1961, p. 40, reports an important summary made by Professor Calvin W. Taylor, of Utah, concerning the relationship of IQ to creativity:

> He cites experiments at various places in the country that have shown that if an IQ test is used to select top level talent, about 70 percent of those who have the highest 20 percent of the scores on a creativity test battery will be missed.
>
> Traditional intelligence tests, he says, cover only a very few of the fifty or more dimensions of the mind that have been discovered.
>
> He tells of a test in which the researchers selected twenty-eight dimensions of the mind they felt were relevant to success in a job in the physical sciences. Scientists then were asked to arrange those characteristics in order of rank in terms of importance to the job.
>
> "Traditional intelligence tests have included about five or six of these characteristics, such as general reasoning, vocabulary ability, number ability, memory for ideas, ability to visualize spatially and, perhaps, perceptual speed," he comments. "All but one of these traditional intelligence factors ranked below twentieth in the list."
>
> That is, nineteen out of the twenty characteristics considered by scientists most important on the job in science were not included in the traditional IQ tests. Examples of these top characteristics were intellectual flexibilities, fluencies, originality, penetration, redefinition ability, and sensitivity to problems.

kin, Research Director of the Textile Workers' Union of America, has said that he has seen a number of wage incentive schemes that seemed to him foolproof, with no way of adapting them so that they would benefit the workers. But he has never seen a plan that in practice could not be adapted or "jimmied" in their favor. He reports that a number of times he had objected to management proposals for incentive plans as unfavorable to the workers, only to be told by the men involved, "Don't worry, we'll figure out how to jimmy it." He, himself, could not see any possibility for manipulation of the scheme, yet in every case, within a year, the men in the shop had been able to figure out ways of "beating the system" that he, an expert, could not envision. We are not discussing the ethics of the actions, but the creativity manifested.

We have frequently observed children in deprived neighborhoods playing basketball by tying a fruit basket, with the bottom removed, to a fire escape. This requires a fair amount of creative ingenuity.

ACTION IMPLICATIONS

As a result of the reevaluation of the standard IQ tests and their particular limitations for underprivileged children, a number of recommendations have come forth:

1. One suggestion is to employ performance tests wherever possible, since these appear to be less affected by the vocabulary limitations of the deprived child. Unfortunately, while these tests have a number of advantages, their use does not overcome the problems of rapport, motivation, and test-taking skill encountered with underprivileged youngsters.

2. Davis and Eels have developed a "culture fair" games test which in many ways seems more appropriate for underprivileged groups. While some deprived individuals fare better on this test, others do not. The prob-

lems of rapport, motivation, and practice appear here
again, although the motivation problem is partially reduced by making the test a game.

3. Murray and others have suggested that the deficiencies of the standard IQ tests be corrected. He feels that
the tests are potentially valuable tools and rejects the
argument advanced by some that they should be discarded because of their weaknesses. Not only can the
tests be improved, but different dimensions of intelligence can be tapped. Items employed need not be brief;
tasks showing no change with age can be utilized; time
limits may be removed or lengthened; less academic,
bookish problems can be employed; the thinking involved in solving the problems can be evaluated along
with the accuracy of the final answer; items that discriminate between deprived and middle-class groups can be
removed from the tests, just as items discriminating between the sexes are removed in test construction;* emo-
tionally loaded items can be selected and the responses
to them compared with the more value-free items. These
are just a few of the possible changes that might be introduced to strengthen the tests.

4. Haggard's study, in which the measured IQ of deprived children was raised considerably with only three
hours of special training, highlights the need for giving
these children directed practice, and developing new
test-taking habits. Deprived children are less test conscious and are not accustomed to being evaluated. They
have poor auditory habits, do not concentrate sufficiently
on the examiner's instructions, do not pick up the examinations readily, and, in general, are lethargic, apathetic,
and ill at ease in the test situation. Sometimes they hurry
through the test, just to get it over with and to remove

*It is fairly typical in IQ test construction either to retain only
the items which do not show a sex difference statistically, or to
balance the items so that each sex is favored equally.

themselves from the situation. Some deprived children are more serious about the test, but they are usually over-cautious, anxious and slow.

Simple, undirected practice in test-taking will not over-come these difficulties. In the course of their school ca-reers, deprived youngsters receive much practice, but it is unmotivated, meaningless practice. Experience is a good teacher only when one knows what to learn from it; by itself, practice can merely reinforce bad habits.

5. Haggard's research also demonstrates the great need for rapport. Haggard trained his examiners so that they would know how to work with deprived youngsters. This kind of training is decisive for clinicians and teach-ers. The clinician has to know how to elicit questions from the deprived child, and how to provide answers in terms that are clearly understood, are repeated often, with numerous examples. He must realize that simply giving the child the test instructions, and having him nod that they are understood, is by no means any guarantee. Deprived children, unless they are at ease with the exam-iner, are much more likely to be passive in the test situa-tion.

Rapport is also dependent upon the examiner having confidence that the child *can* do well. In a sense, the clinician has to convey to the deprived child that he un-derstands why the child has not done well in the past, but that now the conditions are different and the child will therefore be able to show his real ability. This should not be false or artificial; in fact, the examiner should believe this and let the child perceive his optimistic, but not de-manding or pressing, expectation.

6. The teacher might choose to ignore the standard IQ results because of the limitations of the test, and instead attempt to discover the "hidden IQ" of the deprived child. This can best be done by noting the child's contri-butions in discussing a topic which interests him a good deal, such as popular music or the world series. Role-

playing (acting out situations) and physical tasks in general are useful for estimating his potential intelligence.

A good deal of the behavior of underprivileged individuals outside the school context indicates considerable intelligence in terms of dealing with problems and interests close to their own lives. Their intelligence is more fully shown in games such as dominoes, in sports, in humor, and in gossip. They are often surprisingly perceptive in sensing various subtle forms of discrimination and the children demonstrate much misdirected ingenuity in avoiding truant officers and the law. In general, it might be said that they are rather "human smart," and their "hidden IQs" are best seem in their human relations.

About the Contributors

ALAN GARTNER is professor of education, Queens College, codirector of the New Human Services Institute, and publisher of *Social Policy*. He is author of *Paraprofessionals and Their Performance*, coauthor of *Children Teach Children*, and coauthor of the forthcoming *The Service Society*.

COLIN GREER is executive editor of *Social Policy*, a senior staff member of the New Human Services Institute, and author of *The Great School Legend*. Formerly, he was director of the University Without Walls at Staten Island Community College.

FRANK RIESSMAN is professor of education, Queens College, codirector of the New Human Services Institute, and editor of *Social Policy*. He is the author of *The Culturally Deprived Child*, coauthor of *Children Teach Children*, and coauthor of the forthcoming *The Service Society*.

STANLEY ARONOWITZ teaches at Staten Island Community College and the New School for Social Research. He is the author of *False Promises: The Shaping of American Working Class Consciousness*.

SAMUEL BOWLES is associate professor of economics at Harvard University. In the Fall, 1974, he and Herbert Gintis will join the Department of Economics, University of Massachusetts (Amherst).

NOAM CHOMSKY is Ferrari P. Ward Professor of Linguistics at the Massachusettes Institute of Technology. His most recent book is *For Reasons of State*.

ROSS EVANS is associate professor of psychology at the University of Wisconsin (Madison) and a staff researcher at the Waisman Center on Mental Retardation and Human Development.

HERBERT GINTIS is assistant professor of economics at Harvard University.

JEROME KAGAN is professor of human development at Harvard University and the author of *Change and Continuity in Infancy* and *Understanding Children*.

DAVID MCCLELLAND is professor of psychology at Harvard University.

GEORGE PURVIN teaches social studies at Manhasset High School, Long Island, New York.